D0284568

EVERYTHING I KNOW ABOUT BUSINESS I LEARNED AT McDONALD'S

EVERYTHING I KNOW ABOUT BUSINESS I LEARNED AT McDONALD'S

THE 7 LEADERSHIP PRINCIPLES THAT DRIVE BREAK OUT SUCCESS

Paul Facella
with Adina Genn

New York Chicago San Fransisco Lisbon London Madrid Mexico City
Milan New Delhi San Juan Seoul Singapore Sydney Toronto

Copyright © 2009 by Paul Facella. All rights reserved. Printed in the United States of America. Except as permitted under the United States Copyright Act of 1976, no part of this publication may be reproduced or distributed in any form or by any means, or stored in a database or retrieval system, without prior written permission of the publisher.

1 2 3 4 5 6 7 8 9 0 DOC/DOC 0 1 4 3 2 1 0 9 8

ISBN: 978-0-07-160141-2
MHID: 0-07-160141-4

This publication is designed to provide accurate and authoritative information in regard to the subject matter covered. It is sold with the understanding that the publisher is not engaged in rendering legal, accounting, or other professional service. If legal advice or other expert assistance is required, the services of a competent professional person should be sought.
  —From a Declaration of Principles Jointly Adopted by a Committee of the American Bar Association and a Committee of Publishers and Associations

McGraw-Hill books are available at special quantity discounts to use as premiums and sales promotions, or for use in corporate training programs. To contact a representative, please visit the Contact Us pages at www.mhprofessional.com.

This book is printed on acid-free paper.

Contents

Foreword by Ed Rensi

Of my 40-plus years in business, 33 were spent at McDonald's, 14 of which I served as president and CEO of the USA division. There, I saw unbelievable strategic leadership, motivation, and inspiration at play every single day. I was surrounded by people who taught me something new nearly every day. And I had the privilege of being mentored by Ray Kroc, a true visionary, and Fred Turner, the operations genius who created an organization that could replicate success and best practices.

What made McDonald's so wildly triumphant? If you'd have asked me this question 15 years ago, I might have answered "standards." But, having retired in 1999, I now view that question with a measure of objectivity. I look at strategic rather than tactical things. It wasn't the Big Mac that drove McDonald's success. It was the auspicious leadership that had the courage to say, "okay let's give it a try"—"it" being the introduction of something new, whether it was Chicken McNuggets, innovative equipment, an enhanced breakfast menu, or an expansion of the drive-thru concept. The company had the systems in place to support such innovation. It delivered messaging—"QSC": quality, service, and cleanliness—that everyone in the organization could easily wrap their arms around. It had great talent. We kept our focus on the customer, and that's how we maneuvered miles ahead of the competition. And the driving force behind the organization started with Ray and Fred and has been carried through to today's leadership under current CEO Jim Skinner.

I'm not only proud of the role I played in the company's success, but also grateful to have realized that you can't do anything without people, without teamwork. McDonald's is built on a chassis of growth opportunities, business opportunities, systems, trust, and, yes, fun. And like many other "Evergreens" (alumni of McDonald's retirees) these elements resonate with me still. I've brought these essentials to one of my great passions, auto racing. As the owner of a leading NASCAR Nationwide Series racing team, Team Rensi Motorsports, I still practice the McDonald's commonsense business approach. In my McDonald's days, I looked at the organization's corporate employees, franchisees, and vendors as partners. And I do the same with Team Rensi, whether I'm collaborating with the administrative staff, crew, the guys in the shop, or sponsors. Together, our work is inspirational and enjoyable.

I first met Paul Facella back in the early 1970s. Like me, Paul began his tenure at McDonald's as crew, working on the restaurant floor back in 1966. Both of us were grillmen, and we never forgot our roots in the daily operations of our business. Paul rose through the organization, ultimately running the New York region, growing it to $600 million in revenues and one of the top-performing regions in the country consistently during the time that I ran the USA division. Paul was the perfect guy, living in the perfect place, running the region right with the perfect group of operators. A New Yorker through and through, he knew the territory and its challenges better than any of us. He built an extraordinary team of licensees and staff. Was he flawless? No, none of us were. But he did whatever needed doing when it needed to be done. And when I pushed, you can be sure he had the courage to question if he believed it was the right thing to do. It's what the region required: someone who understood the culture, who understood the market, and was tough enough to push back.

Ask anyone who ever served at McDonald's about the organization's success and the profound impact it has made on his or her life and you will get just one person's perspective. Ask another person, and another after that, and you inevitably gather points of view that may or may not vary. Collectively, these opinions tell a story and add insight into McDonald's legacy.

Paul was the right person to gather these insights, and in doing so, he won many willing supporters. Perhaps that's because Paul has always understood people, and always inspired their trust. I'm glad Paul wrote this book, and believe it represents hundreds of us, both licensee, corporate, and suppliers that grew in such a great environment.

Paul extracted seven principles he learned from McDonald's: honesty and integrity, courage, relationships, recognition, communication, standards, and leading by example. They represent good business practices—you cannot run a business without those things being in proper order. And they represent Paul, who has demonstrated these elements since the day I met him. Paul remains a terrific confidant—someone whom I am proud to call my friend.

Ed Rensi, former president of McDonald's USA for 14 years, NASCAR team owner

Acknowledgments

In any project, there is a group effort and this book was no different. I am indebted to many individuals for their help and support in this project. What started out as a small self-published book on management principles to use with our clients, turned into a much larger project than I could have imagined. Luckily, I had many people to help and assist me, but more importantly, they are the ones who really helped to write the bulk of this book.

Adina Genn has been a great partner to work with on this project. Her command of the language and ability to say what I was thinking proved tremendous. Maureen, my wife, and Lindsay O'Conner, my administrative assistant, have been so supportive of the project and were invaluable in transcribing all of the interviews—more than 400 pages! Mary Glenn, editorial director, and Ann Pryor, senior publicist from McGraw-Hill have been wonderful to work with. Our agent, Bob Diforio, was instrumental in steering this project along. And, a special thanks goes out to Bob Waldman for his insights.

When the project first came to light, and I realized that I needed some help from the McDonald's corporation, I turned to Fred Turner for his assistance. After explaining my dilemma, he heartily endorsed the project, and in his typical way, got the train going for me. We spent many hours together and besides providing great insights about the company, he also gave me the gift of so much of his personal time—it was a real pleasure working with him.

My thanks goes to all of the individuals who helped in this project by allowing an interview, a conversation, or lending support by pointing me in the right direction when I needed it most. Jim Skinner, Don Thompson, Jeff Stratton, Bob Marshall, Rich Floersch, Kathy May, Vivian Ross, Pat Harris, Jack Daly, Susan Clark-McBride, Michael Bullington, Al Golin, Joyce Molinaro, Barb Balle, and Fred Turner. Although I have been gone from the corporation for eight years, it was as if I was still a part of the McFamily, and I was treated so well by so many.

The group of former McDonald's employees was just terrific as well, lending their ideas and thoughts whenever I asked. I could have spent another year just listening to their stories and the passion that they had for the system. I spoke with everyone who I thought could contribute in some way, and had to pare down the list to make it manageable. No one turned me down, and they could not have been more gracious in sharing their past with me. Regardless of the issues surrounding each one leaving the company, everyone seemed to feel privileged to have been associated with McDonald's. Mike Roberts summed it up for everyone I spoke with in saying, "No matter what the circumstances, I am proud to have been a part of it." My thanks to Mike Roberts, Frank Behan, Ed Rensi, Bob Weissmueller, Tom Dentice, John and Marge Cooke, Claire Babrowski, Debra Koenig, Mike Quinlan, Paul Schrage, Don Horowitz, Jack Greenberg, Donn Wilson, Matt Seigel, David Delgado, Bob Vidor, Jan Kramer, Burt Cohen, Ernie Annibale, and Willis Smart.

The heart of the company, the licensees who operate 85 percent of the restaurants within the system, were equally supportive. Their stories and comments were great support for the validation of the principles on which I based this book. Ron Bailey, Jim Lewis, Paul Hendel, Sam Munroe, Tony Liedtke, Sam Samaha, Rick McCoy, Sal Baglieri, Joe Liegeois, Roland Jones, Irv Klein, and Rick Yandoli were all great in their comments to me.

Our supplier network was there as well to lend its assistance to me. I am grateful to Frank Kuchuris, Peter Grimm, Pat Paterno, and Ted Perlman for their help.

I also want to personally acknowledge four wonderful women who over a span of 26 years, the time I spent working directly for McDonald's corporation, assisted me in so many ways, far beyond what the title of administrative assistant belies. Anyone who has been in management knows the value of a great administrative assistant, and I was fortunate to have four of them. Their unwavering support and guidance during the years that I learned how to navigate the issues that arose, is truly appreciated. Patrice Tryman, Toni DiBlasio, Toni Liegeois, and Mary Calabro...my thanks.

Of course, there is one woman whose support and advice proved to be vital in my success with the corporation. I met her when I was 18 and working the grill at McDonald's. She ordered her hamburger plain, with no onions or pickles, and she still does . . . that woman is my wife, Maureen. With her quiet and gentle demeanor, she gained the respect of the corporate staff and the owner/operators within the region. I can honestly say that without her, this career would not have been, and I for one, am truly grateful.

There are also a few people who were very influential to me during my career as well as those previously mentioned. Unfortunately they have since passed away, but I want to remember them as well: Dan Radice, Mike Young, Lou Damiano, Andy Savastano, and Jim Cantalupo. They have all helped me in numerous ways, and their friendship was warmly felt.

Introduction

On February 15, 1966, store number 768 opened in a typical suburban New York town on Long Island. It was an average winter day, 42 degrees and clear, and, as was done with most McDonald's stores at the time, the opening was held on a Tuesday. It was a "red-and-white"-style store identical to the hundreds before it that were beginning to dot the U.S. landscape. The store opened with reasonable sales, and within seven months, on Labor Day weekend, I began working there as a bright-eyed, eager 16-year-old.

Like thousands before me, I found my position at McDonald's to be my first real job. In 1966, McDonald's had a total of $219 million in sales from its 862 restaurants. Thirty-four years later, when I retired from McDonald's, the company had reached sales of more than $40 billion and a total store count of more than 28,707 units worldwide.

This is my story, though there are thousands of individuals like me who benefited, grew, and had the privilege of working in this intriguing system called McDonald's. And although my career took me to many places, it primarily was about my experiences in the New York metropolitan region. Some of us became managers and supervisors, some middle managers, some corporate executives, and some suppliers or franchisees within the system. And some left to go on to other fields of success. Some may have been promoted too quickly. Some missed the opportunities. Some burned out. Yet many succeeded in leaving a positive mark. Most of us learned on the job: by doing, observing, watching, and executing; by trial and error. And, to a person, it seems, they all mostly enjoyed their experiences with the system.

I was indeed privileged to have served at the company at such an auspicious time. It was unique. It was exciting. It was challenging. And it was a wonderful learning experience for all of us who were able to take the opportunity afforded to us at the time. The company, now in its fifty-third year, is the most successful restaurant organization in the world, and one of the most recognized brands in the world. This is a compilation of one person's firsthand observations and thoughts on how McDonald's grew into the organization it is today: what it was like to play a role in its growth, how it felt, how it all transpired, and how it influenced my personal growth and thousands of others. I truly believe that most of us would not have achieved the successes we experienced at McDonald's had it not been for the spirit of team that we encountered in our early careers. The system molded many of us, average individuals, both company employees and franchisees, and made us much more than many of us ever dreamed we could be.

My story stems from various personal viewpoints. I was a crewperson. I worked for a licensee of the system. I was a store manager and a director of operations. Later, I joined the corporation and worked midmanagement jobs in training and operations, until finally I became a regional vice president, and during the course of 12 years, was responsible for more than 450 stores and $600 million in sales. While those numbers are important, they don't tell the whole story. The story of friendships and frustrations; the missed opportunities and the mistakes made; the on-the-job training we received and our wide-eyed innocence at times; and of the many vignettes that transpired over those years that are still vivid and important to many of the people who were present at that time.

While the perspective of insights and conclusions inside this book is mine, it was validated and supported by the over-whelming majority of interviews I conducted. I was fortunate in that everyone whom I attempted to contact to interview for this book went out of his or her way to help. I was able to speak with an incredible group of individuals. I am grateful for those people who shared their stories and thoughts with me during this journey. And with that spirit of team, and collaboration, they gave substance to this story about one person's career with the McDonald's organization. Interestingly, everyone I inter-viewed, even those who have left the company, still refer to McDonald's as "our" or "my" company. Like me, they may have left the system, and yet the system is still with them.

In my quest to shed insight into those years, I wanted to uti-lize the "three-legged stool" concept—symbolizing the collabo-ration between McDonald's owner/operators, suppliers, and corporate staff—that has always served as the foundation of the organization. Together, the three units teamed up as partners, moving the brand and the organization forward—this alliance is a critical component to McDonald's success. And I wanted to be true to that concept and seek input from all three sources to support my conclusions. It wasn't difficult.

Whatever success I achieved has been far eclipsed by many of the others I had the pleasure of working with, and all of us had the benefit of serving within McDonald's hugely successful sys-tem. All of us believe that McDonald's system did a lot right—a whole lot right, again and again, year after year. But there were some dark times as well. At one point the company almost went bankrupt; in another instance, the operators formed an organization to challenge the corporation on some of its policies; in still another, Fred Turner himself was ready to leave and become an operator; over the years customers protested the brand in a number of ways; and on more than one occasion an executive was asked to leave. While there were glitches and mistakes made during those 53 years—some of them more harmful than others—the system righted itself and kept going. And that is the true test of a successful organization.

George Will stated in 1997, when writing about owner/operators, that "McDonald's has made more millionaires, and especially black and Hispanic millionaires, than any other economic entity ever, anywhere." And while this isn't news to those who follow McDonald's, they may not realize that hundreds of company employees, myself included, along with suppliers, enjoyed the same incredible success. But it didn't stop there. Second- and now third-generation owner/operators as well as suppliers have benefited. And the success we speak about is not necessarily the monetary kind. Ray Kroc summed up what many people whom I interviewed told me:

Success to me is happiness. But what I mean by happiness is probably different from its everyday meaning to most people. To me, happiness is a by-product of achievement.

To us, success really was about the fun and excitement and satisfaction that we felt from accomplishing much of what we set out to do. Those familiar with McDonald's corporate history over the years already know about the perfect storm that hit the system. Literally four years ago, the night before the opening general session of McDonald's 2004 Worldwide Convention, Jim Cantalupo, the CEO at the time, suddenly passed away. This was a devastating blow to the organization, as Jim was in the midst of executing the "Plan to Win" strategy. Charlie Bell, another crew alumnus from Australia and executive at the time, was quickly put into the position. But in an uncanny and terrible turn of events, he tragically succumbed to cancer only nine months later. Jim Skinner was placed in the position, only the eighth CEO in the company's entire history of over 50 years. Jim, a veteran of the system and crew alumni as well, took the reins, keeping the momentum and driving growth to new heights.

How many organizations could sustain such losses and not only promote completely from within, but also keep the momentum and leadership intact? And here's another thought to ponder: The current management team for the most part never had a personal relationship with Ray Kroc, the founder of present-day McDonald's, and yet, his vision, passion, and ideals are still very much evident today. How have his values and mission lived on with each successive generation of executives? And what principles can be shared for others to replicate?

There must be something to the system after all. To many of us, and you'll read this again and again in the pages that follow, the system served as an extension of family—or what we called the McFamily. The name alone says a lot. And this family cared not about your pedigree, or your heritage, or experience, but allowed your development and growth to grasp the available opportunities. It became a haven where many of us could succeed and gain the self-confidence that we may have lacked initially. It nurtured, honed, and developed the skills we would need to be successful. And the skills also transferred to other careers and occupations from individuals who went on to other ventures, still mindful of the impact of their early development within the system of McDonald's.

Despite its global presence, McDonald's for many years was not the kind of firm that might be covered in the *Harvard Business Review* as the latest in organizational development. In fact, in the early years, those with higher education were in some ways shunned. Ray Kroc never graduated from high school. Most of the executives in the early years and throughout the history of the company had a remarkable lack of formal education—though many of the leadership, including former CEO Mike Quinlan did earn college degrees, and in some cases graduate degrees. We were an eclectic group, with amazingly diverse backgrounds, including military credentials, blue-collar skills, and so on—and most of us had little if any previous restaurant experience. There was no bias overall, just a penchant for *getting the job done.* Yet the idea of organizational charts, well, as Honorary Chairman Fred Turner—Ray's direct protégé—told me, "We built the organizational chart around their talents." Again, it's not something you would hear about in the latest management book on organizations. But perhaps it's something to consider in reviewing your own organizational structure.

But that never seemed to matter. While grandiose plans and formal organizational charts were not the norm, the system developed a tenacious work ethic and a laserlike focus on being the best experience to the customer. Through sheer passion and determination, the organization created a culture second to none in the industry. It attracted the kind of individuals who enjoyed this results-driven culture and blossomed in this environment. These folks stayed on, to long-tenured careers within the organization. And these core principles, which we will review, are relevant in other organizations today as well.

That drive propelled McDonald's into the big leagues, pushing us insiders into situations we could never have imagined. Take this anecdote from former zone manager Frank Behan: "We were at a Coca-Cola/McDonald's convention one time, and you know I'm not an educated guy. And I didn't follow the news perhaps as much as I should have, so I wasn't really up on current events. Once your head is stuck in McDonald's, it's like you can't get it out, you know. So anyway we're down in California. And they're bringing in speakers like the ex-prime minister of England. I'm in over my head—I know that I don't belong in this group. So I was asked, 'How come you don't ask a question?' I responded, 'I guess because I can't think of one to ask.' And I was told to ask a question tomorrow. But I had none. So it was brought up to Fred Turner, the CEO at the time, who says, 'You know we bring our guys out and you know we want them to participate like the Coca-Cola guys. I said the Coca-Cola guys all went to Harvard and Yale. Your guys went to HU [Hamburger University, which trains thousands of McDonald's employees].'" Maybe it embarrassed the top executives that regular guys like Frank didn't ask questions. But we were who we were. And we delivered where it really counted—on the restaurant floor, with sales and customer satisfaction. We weren't cut from the same cloth as those at the Ivy Leagues, but because of what we achieved eventually even *Harvard Business Review* began to pay attention to us, as you will read later in these pages.

Fred Turner has always said that *the whole is greater than the sum of its parts*, and that pretty well depicts McDonald's. And yet, the sailing was not always smooth. In an organization where there are big egos and big personalities, everyone didn't always get along, and there were plenty of petty quibbles. And there were also some hard times. Every operator wasn't guaranteed to be the biggest and most successful one. Every company person did not make officer. As former vice president Willis Smart recalled to me: "It is not necessarily a place for everyone. If it is for you, it is a great place to be, and it gives *very average people an opportunity to accomplish incredible things, and usually at a pretty young age.*" Well said, and heart-felt by many people I interviewed.

The structure of the three-legged stool was such that we were all partners in the system together, and together we always pulled through, even in the darkest times.

Was there a grand design, a master strategy behind McDonald's growth? No, I think not. But there was a conscious effort to continually improve and be the best. It grew organically from within. The kernels of the organization were planted by Fred and Ray. And they are still alive and well today within the organization, in a different way, by different people, but the kernels are there. In fact, Jim Skinner, the current CEO, carries on with a new strategy that reflects the core principles and that is updated to remain relevant and viable in today's business environment.

I began writing this book as a result of my post-McDonald's tenure, which in the past eight years included consulting, with my group, to various organizations. In this role, my staff and I kept returning to the basics of leadership, management, culture, and vision issues—concepts familiar to anyone in business. Yet, many of our clients struggle with them, failing to see how simple the basics really are and the role they play in building a thriving organization. As I strived to articulate to clients how organizations build from within, I returned again and again to the core ideology that I learned at McDonald's. I felt that the principles I learned at McDonald's, in their simplicity, might be beneficial for others in growing their organizations. I don't claim to be a final authority on management. I offer only what I witnessed. And what I witnessed seemed fairly simple and straightforward to me, and it still does. You'll find no fancy charts or big acronyms here—just telling what seemed right, the commonsense approach to larger issues and trying to do the right thing with people; that approach seemed to work.

So my quest was to transfer what I learned from the system into simple language that was clear and actionable for all management levels. In my consulting practice, we like to reduce these principles to three keys: *People, Environment,* and *Direction.* Ironically, these are the basics I learned on the restaurant floor. As a store manager, the roles and behaviors of immediate assistant managers and crew were no different from the department heads and staff I worked with years later as an officer. In fact, most complexities I saw at the officer level were often no different from the challenges faced by operators, managers, and crew on the restaurant floor. The same principles applied. And the truth be told, I wasn't alone in my observation of this. You will read about a number of former executives in other organizations now, and how those principles have helped them in their current leadership positions.

You may notice that in these pages I and others refer to "owner/operators," "licensees," and "franchisees" interchangeably. They are one and the same. McDonald's is built on a system of involved owners—entrepreneurs who follow the company's standards and who are active in their stores, every day. Those owner/operators who met the system's criteria for expansion qualified for more stores. And multiple operators had to establish a solid midmanagement group of supervision and, in larger organizations, director-level employees, some with ownership interests as well. Still, only the strongest operators could expand, and just like the single-unit licensees, they were required to be involved in day-to-day operations within their organizations. There were no absentee operators, as Ray Kroc noted many years ago, in his own indelible style: "We have a lot of millionaires in our company, but they better not act like millionaires, or they won't be here!"

In writing this book, I incorporated "lessons learned" at appropriate times to help focus key points along the way. I think you will find that many of these learnings can be applied to all organizations, and the concepts and ideas can be replicated.

McDonald's is a very intimate and personable organization, and was especially so in the earlier years. Even today, while interviewing franchisees for this book, I discovered that they are still impressed that they can put a phone call into the CEO or other executive-level officer, and if they cannot get that person within the next hour or two, he or she will return their call usually within 24 hours. While this may seem hard to believe, to this day, with 1.6 million worldwide employees serving more than 50 million customers a day, the organization strives to be family oriented and remain focused and passionate about serving customers. And while the communications are more complicated and the conversations perhaps less frequent, the organization still pushes to stay small, nimble, and responsive to its customers—both to the patrons who visit the restaurants and the thousands of licensees or operators worldwide.

While writing this book, I had the pleasure of attending McDonald's worldwide convention attended by operators, suppliers, and key management—all 13,000 of them! I watched Fred Turner chat with operators, friends, and suppliers nonstop every day; I observed Jim Skinner, the present CEO (who started as crew some 35 years ago) remain accessible and available to everyone present. I saw all senior managers speak with anyone who cared to stop at their booth. Bob Marshall, vice president of U.S. restaurant operations, told me that he was with a group of individuals who were involved with the running of the Chicago restaurant show each year, one of the biggest events in McCormick Center. They were engrossed by the displays and commitment they saw from the suppliers—their partners in the system—who were present. But this was not unusual. This was and is the culture of the organization. It's one with deep-rooted principles of business conduct and a code of values. Do it right;

do it big. Ray Kroc, who opened his first store in 1955, along with his first grill man, Fred Turner, who still remains active behind the scenes, taught us all that we are equals in the organization. Everyone is on a first-name basis, all of us are passionate about what we do, always striving to do it better. It was evident throughout the convention that this culture still prevailed.

As I walked the floor of the exhibit area, meeting and chatting with many longtime friends and operators, I was again struck by the power of many of the principles I describe in this book. At one point, a very successful operator and his wife approached me, and in the course of the conversation, the wife admitted that she had saved "the blouse I wore when you first brought us into the system." And her husband countered with the fact that he still has the piece of paper that we had sent with the directions to get to the regional office. This, 17 years later! Talk about the power of recognition. In another instance, an operator shared with me how much he valued our retreats at the corporate ski lodge, where operators and staff had the chance to get away from the office and store, and reconnect with their passion for the system. He validated the importance of communications and relationships. How great I felt that I could have helped him in some small way. I share that, because all of us in management have the ability to touch and positively influence those whom we work with. It's a great perk of the job, but one that needs to be remembered and respected as well.

Communications, relationships, recognition. These are just some of the principles I include in the book. Others include standards, honesty and integrity, courage, and leading by example. Together, these seven principles are, to my mind, what helped McDonald's grow into the organization it is today. And my premise has been validated by everyone I interviewed for this book, though they often had their own perspective on these seven principles. Together, these principles are *the sum of the parts*, and they reveal the real story behind McDonald's success. They can also serve as the building blocks to grow any organization. You will also notice, in many cases, how these principles are related and even co-dependent with each other. After all, without solid communications, how can we develop a powerful relationship? Without integrity, how can I develop a true and meaningful relationship? I believe you will have your own insights to these areas, and that can only add to their importance in leading an organization. Share them with your teams.

A number of years ago, I attended a convention of real estate people from around the country. I met up with a former McDonald's colleague. As we chatted about family and friends, I asked him what the difference was between his time in McDonald's and now with his present employer, a competitor. He thought for a minute, and then told me, "McDonald's has a soul. The others don't."

I think that perfectly sums up the differences between McDonald's and "all others." I hope to show you some of the soul of the McDonald's organization in these pages, and allow you the opportunity to both understand and perhaps apply some of the principles that came from such a remarkable group of people.

EVERYTHING I KNOW ABOUT BUSINESS I LEARNED AT McDONALD'S

Honesty and Integrity:
All in a Handshake

It's not what you do but the way you do it.

—Ray Kroc

It seems only fitting that honesty and integrity is our first chapter. As Don Thompson, the current president of McDonald's USA, told me: "It's foundational. Everything is built off of that, and if you don't have that one right, you can't move to the other principles."

Ray Kroc put honesty and integrity at McDonald's very core, going against the grain in the food business. In the 1950s and 1960s, an era when the industry was rife with kickbacks—where fast-food chains expected a percentage back from the suppliers selling goods to franchisees—Ray would have none of it. He expanded on the topic of honesty in a speech to a business school in 1974: "Whatever you do, don't prostitute yourself and do something for money. It's got to be in your heart and your soul. You've got to sleep with it and eat it, and it's something you can't live without."

Advocating a system of honesty and integrity—and demanding the same from corporate, franchisees, and vendors—Ray and Fred Turner devised a system whose stakeholders could expect a fair shake. And in many ways the company was ahead of its time. From handshake agreements to the company's ombudsman programs to the no-walls/no-doors layout at the initial and subsequent

Oak Brook, Illinois, home office, all indicators pointed to McDonald's transparency—a culture where doing the right, moral, and ethical thing was important. And that was very deliberate. That culture lives on today. As Don Thompson noted to me: "I tell everybody, there are a lot of things that can be fixed and resolved, but there are three that cannot. Don't lie. Don't cheat. Don't steal. Because if you do any of those, I can't trust you."

Doing It Right

"Ray had seen abuses," Fred Turner recalled. "Tasty Freeze was getting money on the side. Ray was selling mixers and originally ice cream, but then liquid mix and soft serve. And shake mix. So that was his industry, and he saw what they did. And he was convinced that we shouldn't make money off the suppliers. It gives the company a selfish interest and a conflict. He saw that that wasn't healthy, and he didn't want that. So day one, he was saying no kickbacks. "

Willis Smart, former regional vice president and currently an operations vice president with Dunkin Brands, saw integrity as integral to the system. "I believe there was a gentlemen's agreement that we were going to treat each other ethically," Willis told me. "The fact that we didn't get into the distribution business and keep those profits, I think, is an example of us bypassing a growth opportunity on behalf of keeping the relationship with the franchisees to be a very strong one."

Ray's position might be considered unusual even today. But his business acumen would still be spot-on, especially considering the fate of companies that do not put the needs of the franchisee first. Take, for example, Krispy Kreme, a hot company at one point. By 2005 the company saw double-digit losses, and franchisees filed for bankruptcy for a number of reasons, including that they could not pay the company's excessive franchise and supply fees, as reported in the *New York Times*.

In the interest of seeing his operators succeed, Ray even saw that supplier rebates went to the franchisees, not to corporate. He did anything he could to lower costs for the operators and help them be successful. This was a core principle and major point of differentiation from other franchise organizations, even today. In my consulting practice we have worked with a number of franchise companies, and it continues to strike me how in other systems the franchisor is less concerned about the franchisee's financial success, which can result in ultimately compromising the entire system. It seems that many franchisors are concerned only about the royalty check and how many more units a franchisee will develop, *with the franchisee taking all the risks.*

Lesson Learned

As a franchisor, McDonald's ran its system so that all of the stakeholders stood to gain. It made everyone feel like a true partner.

3

Putting the needs of the franchisee first was paramount to building McDonald's, but that didn't make building the system easy. Far from it, said Mike Quinlan, who served as the company's fourth CEO, from 1987 to 1998. Ray was a powerful motivator, an idealist, who struggled to meet his bottom line in the early years. Noted Mike: "Ray used to say, 'The operators have to make money before the company does, right?' Well, his formula was so messed up we were going broke before Sonneborn figured out we were going broke." Mike was referring to Harry Sonneborn, the company's first CEO who brought the company public in 1965; it was Harry who devised the strategy to acquire the land where McDonald's units would be built—putting McDonald's in the real estate business, and opening up a new revenue stream that enabled the company finally to begin to operate profitably.

Still, Ray steered clear of conflicts of interest as he purchased the company from the McDonald brothers, Fred told me. In the fast-food industries, some suppliers "were also cheapening the meat," Fred said, referring to the process of adding more fat to the meat—a verboten practice in a company that rapidly implemented its 100-percent-pure beef, no-additives, no-filler policy.

Ray's foundation of honesty and integrity has permeated the organization ever since. And the evidence exists today with suppliers, in corporate, and on the restaurant floor as the three-legged stool concept, mentioned in the introduction, whose number one commitment remains delivering quality, service, and cleanliness, or QSC, to the customer.

As Bob Marshall, a vice president of McDonald's U.S. restaurant operations, put it: "Do one kickback and that whole principle is out the window. A kickback—when you are operating on integrity—would have thrown the whole thing; you are throwing it all away."

Business on a Handshake

Perhaps the most striking example of McDonald's honesty and integrity is its handshake agreements with vendors. Mostly a thing of the past in virtually every industry, handshake agreements are alive and well with McDonald's suppliers, even in today's litigious society. Many of these suppliers are now second- and third-generation businesses, whose fathers took Ray Kroc at his word.

"I didn't and still don't have a contract," said Frank Kuchuris, CEO and chairman of East Balt Bakery, with bakeries across the United States, Asia, and Europe. Frank's father, Louis, struck a deal with Ray in 1955. "So many people would look the other way when Ray said 15-cent hamburgers," Frank told me. "But when Ray explained the concept, Dad was on board with it. He thought it was such a great thing."

Lynal Root, McDonald's former director of purchasing, was one of the key executives in the early years who got Ray and Fred's modus operandi. He followed in Ray and Fred's footsteps, understanding the importance that honesty and integrity played with the organization, as Peter Grimm, a 35-year supplier to McDonald's, shared with me. "Lynal Root got people to spend billions of dollars building the system, building the capacity of the system, bakeries, wheat plants, distribution centers, taking a chance of moving from Cleveland to Los Angeles, or building a bakery in the U.K. when they had seven stores," Peter noted. "This man did more with a handshake than anybody at most companies does with a contract. Truly incredible. And 85, 90 percent of it was done based on word and on relationships. John Paterakis [Peter's senior partner] tells this story about the time that he first went to McDonald's and they wanted him to build the first automated bakery on the East Coast in Baltimore. He took his lawyer with him and offered Ray and Fred a contract. Ray and Fred said, 'Well there is no point in trying to offer us any contract because any contract you write, you can break. Either we are going to have a relationship with each other that says you are prepared to invest this money and build this bakery for us, or no contract is going to get us comfortable if we aren't comfortable with you as people.' And that was a lesson I have not forgotten." As Peter pointed out, vendors went that extra mile because of the faith they had in McDonald's.

Lynal laid much of the foundation of present-day McDonald's, and his business practices are evident today, as Bob Marshall, who had worked closely with Lynal, explains. "The whole idea that we could operate this long on a handshake agreement as opposed to signed contracts, it really attests to the fact that we have to have honesty and we have to have integrity," Bob told me. "And I think that with McDonald's and being as complex as we are, we are actually pretty simple in the aspect of what you see is what you get. And there is not a lot of unnecessary depth that goes with it, and I see it in interesting ways. You know, people that are honest and have integrity tend to be open, so I go into a McDonald's Worldwide Convention recently, and there are 13,000 people, of which probably about 4,000 are suppliers, and they hear exactly the same thing that the company people hear, they hear exactly the same thing that operators are hearing. So I think there is a transparency there that you can only get when you are honest. If you weren't, you would have different messages for different constituencies. And I think that the fact there is the openness and the honesty and the transparency really makes it pretty interesting. I go into meetings frequently and I'll sit down, and there will be regional people, there will be suppliers there, there will be operators there, and there's lots of times that if you didn't know better, you wouldn't know who is who," Bob said, referring to the typical McDonald's environment where all the stakeholders are truly treated as equal partners. He added: "And the only way you could do that is by being open and honest."

Those I spoke to agreed readily with Bob. Consider for example, the perspective of Jeff Stratton, McDonald's chief restaurant officer. "The honesty and integrity that has been part of the culture of our company in my 35 years has really never changed," Jeff told me. "I think throughout the course of my experience with the company, whether it has been with Fred, to Mike [Quinlan], to Ed [Rensi], to Jim [Skinner], the honesty and integrity is something I think we have consistently been able to hang our hat on. We are a principled company and one that believes in doing things in a right and proper way, and I think there are a million examples of doing that, from the supplier relationship side of the equation, and the way that we have always talked we still do today. There is nothing wrong with making sure our suppliers are healthy and making a good return on their investment in McDonald's as well as demanding a terrific price generated because of our size at the back door for our restaurants."

Leaps of Faith Driven by Values

Ray Kroc was the consummate salesperson, as former chief franchise officer Burt Cohen explained: "You'd go into his office and sit down, and he'd have the most harebrained idea, but after five minutes you'd say, 'Let's get started.' He could convince anybody." But as Burt pointed out, Ray's "passion and commitment to a set of values" was always evident. And that proved vital in getting good people on board. And that inspired those handshake agreements. Again and again.

Suppliers had faith in the company, whose leaders pushed up their shirtsleeves—much the way they have always done on the restaurant floor—showing them precisely how to meet the company's strict standards. Whether it was cultivating potatoes or producing beef, suppliers saw a real partner in McDonald's and had no qualms investing hundreds of thousands of dollars to build plants in order to properly honor the handshake agreements. It was a two-way commitment. Ray demanded their integrity, and the implicit message was that he would stand by them so long as they followed McDonald's rigorous standards. They not only followed, they developed the technology to ensure food safety and quality, catering to McDonald's buying patterns, ultimately adopting the highest industry standards and certifications. "Suppliers were trusted to voluntarily meet food standards set by McDonald's and they lived up to corporate expectations," noted retired senior vice president John Cooke.

And it inspired first-rate results, for both McDonald's and the suppliers, who in the spirit of growth collaborated as partners.

"I remember a meat supplier in Columbus, Ohio—Larry Frank—who started out in a little meat market, a little one-cylinder automatic, who really grew big and who had that relationship with McDonald's, and his quality was just so great," Tom Dentice, a retired executive vice president, told me.

Harold Kestenbaum, a well-known franchise attorney and author on the subject, who is of counsel to Ruskin Moscou Faltischek in New York, believes that McDonald's honesty and integrity lay the foundation for a solid partnership between corporate and vendors—a quality that franchisees have always appreciated. This partnership translates to better economies of scale and, ultimately, pricing. "I'm not sure other franchisors haven't copied the McDonald's system," he said. "McDonald's doesn't have to put out an ad for franchisees. People want them. A McDonald's franchise—it's like gold."

The suppliers' growth spoke volumes about McDonald's integrity. Later, as the company moved from individual bakers to dedicated regional McDonald's suppliers, it "immediately started to establish that same solid relationship with the new suppliers," Tom said. "In Ohio, where I was at the time, when we went to a single-purpose bakery, these folks spent millions of dollars to put up that bakery on a handshake. Think about that."

Lesson Learned

Conduct your operation with honesty and integrity, and vendors will put their faith in you—perhaps even take risks with you because you have won them over. These partnerships can generate the kinds of results where the organization, and all the stakeholders involved, stand to benefit. It's a win-win situation.

That leap of faith was not limited to vendors. Consider the would-be franchisees who vie to invest hundreds of thousands of dollars of their savings to become an owner/operator. They must first devote a significant amount of hours over the course of as much as two years in training—without knowing for sure that they will ultimately be awarded a restaurant. There are no guarantees, and yet each year an estimated 7,000 prospects inquire about the chance to become owner/operators, despite the rigorous training requirements. It is a grueling process to get certified. Only about 1 percent eventually make it to becoming owner/operators with their first store.

And while the franchisees do have contractual agreements, it is their faith that the company will do right by them that largely drives their success. Former McDonald's U.S. and global president Mike Roberts said that faith dates back to the beginning of McDonald's history. "The early operator base remembered the days when Ray stayed in their homes and the company had very little money, and it was all based on 'we have to help each other,'" Mike told me. "Those early operators, I think, are still the reason today that the company is doing well, because that solid support was based on commitments that individuals make, not based on a licensing agreement. You can't force people to act based on a licensing agreement." Operators from day one knew that the company had their best interests at heart, and knew that Ray wasn't out to hurt them, Mike added.

That integrity—the promise to do right by the operator in order to best serve the customer—was a given within the company. "It was all about obligations and keeping the focus of everybody's attention on the restaurant," Mike pointed out. Everyone in the system shares the same interest: supporting the restaurant as it pertains to the customer. Mike reminded me that those in the purchasing department are known to phone the folks in the field eager to know how to help with the customer

9

experience. Those in construction ask how they can help with the look and feel of the restaurants. And those in operations press to learn what they can do to work with the restaurants in better executing and planning. "This is my one takeaway of this organization's success," Mike said.

Owner/operators found the spirit of trust worked both ways. "Based on their reported sales they paid their rent and service fees," noted John Cooke. "There was very little auditing by the company."

In my own region, we conducted very few audits on operators, and when we did, rarely did I ever find any major discrepancies. Anything we did find was usually the product of an oversight in recordkeeping rather than cash theft. Even in the scarce instances when I suspected foul play, I found nothing. It was a tribute to the honesty in how our operators conducted themselves.

Trust and faith were also prevalent on the vendor side. As Peter Grimm told me: "I think back all the years I have been involved with supply chain, it's almost impossible to remember any incident where anyone we were involved with ever got in trouble because they did something under the table or off the books. And when you consider the volumes or amounts of money that is involved in some of these transactions, that is a staggering thing."

Honesty and integrity continue to play a big role in the company's values and core principles, as current CEO Jim Skinner told me. "One only has to look at the paper today. Every day there is someone going to jail because they couldn't control themselves, and so you have to ask yourself, were they genuinely honest people with integrity before they were there?" he pointed out. "It is a big factor with me, and if I find people that are dealing from the bottom of the deck or have motivation other than the system motivation, and all of that, and do just disingenuous things, to me that's a deal breaker."

No Free Hamburgers

Early in my career, I saw that honesty and integrity were one of the founding principles of the company and, by and large, permeated the organization down to the smallest detail. Ed Rensi, a former burger flipper who went on to serve as president and CEO of McDonald's USA, put it to me this way: "You can call my wife right now and ask her this question. When Ed was a store manager, did he ever give you a free hamburger? Ask her. She still talks about it. Because I would not under any circumstances take anything from the company."

Still, many of us faced the pressure to give out free food. We found ingenious ways to combat that. When I was a manager, crew kids were challenged by friends for gratis hamburgers. I'd reach into my pocket and hand the kids a dollar, offering to buy them a burger. They got the message, and in most cases it embarrassed them in front of their friends and peers.

Honesty and integrity were a natural to Ed, and he saw those qualities all around him. "It was the culture, so it made it a lot easier," he said. "Fred had an abundance of common sense, and that is what honesty and integrity is all about. Common sense—the [ability to distinguish the] difference . . . between right and wrong. Fred Turner had it, and he made sure we all had it. Fred expected a certain level of behavior, and he got it. And Fred would not put dishonesty around him."

But unlike, say, standards, which can be taught, honesty and integrity are innate—you either have it, or you don't. As Willis Smart stated to me, "I always go back to honesty and integrity being something that you don't talk about . . . you just do." Former McDonald's zone manager Frank Behan offered this perspective: "It's how you view yourself. There are people that are honest to a certain degree but then can be bought past that degree, and then they're no longer honest."

11

The system had no room for those who abused Ray's founding principles—and incidents were rare. Paper distributor Ted Perlman noted that "some of the people that misused the trust were for the most part good people at all levels who might have been misguided but meant well. There were four or five more senior people that misused the trust, but those were exceptions not the rule."

Incidents of corruption are so rare at McDonald's that when I did encounter it, it took me several moments to recognize it at face value. Back when I was a director of operations for the company, I was approached by a contractor who, after completing the construction of several new restaurants, was eager for more business. And because we were always building and refurbishing units, we were on the constant lookout for quality contractors who could get the job done. No single source could handle it all. Out in the parking lot, this particular contractor said there would be cash for me for each site going forward. I looked at him, puzzled, so he repeated his offer. I was dumbfounded that he could be so stupid (and that I could be so unsuspecting). I told him we don't do business like that, and he never built another unit for us. I have to believe that scene has been played out many times over the years with McDonald's management.

It might seem naïve to believe that everyone at McDonald's shared my ethics, but I'm not the only one with this perspective. "I think the degree to which integrity permeates the relationship, it's almost as if you don't have that, you can't survive," Peter Grimm added, noting with little wonder that the few who played shenanigans were quickly pushed out of the system. "Rotten eggs stink, and it doesn't take long, in a place where there were very few of them, [for them to] stand out like a sore thumb."

Tom Dentice shared that view. "I could probably count the number of people . . . really weren't honest and didn't have integrity," he told me. "There were some certainly, but I think that was one of the character traits where there was a standard set that was so high, that people that didn't have it washed out, probably without even being fired . . . just couldn't function well and it didn't fit. [They] could never fit in, just weren't really part of the whole system, . . . never got comfortable, and they left. I think that, again, that it was part of our actual culture to be honest and have integrity to do what was right." The company looked for that in our suppliers and franchisees, and expected those behaviors in our employees.

Those who didn't mirror those expectations were sent packing. For example, while serving as a regional vice president back in the 1990s, I caught an owner/operator running unacceptable stores, who'd opened a chicken restaurant directly across the street from his McDonald's unit and used McDonald's product in his chicken restaurant. This was in direct violation of his license agreement. We disenfranchised him.

13

Food for Thought
How Can You Promote Honesty and Integrity in Your Own Organization?

Not only must you walk the talk, so must everyone you work with, whether he or she is a colleague, vendor, or partner. While honest people as a rule tend to attract like-minded people, keep in mind that you will on occasion encounter someone unscrupulous. Sever ties with that person. That individual—as well as others in the organization—will get the message loud and clear that you will not tolerate dishonesty in your organization.

A One-of-a-Kind Ombudsman Program

In the spirit of wanting to do right by McDonald's stakeholders, the company in 1974 launched its ombudsman program, widely believed to be the first of its kind in the industry, where owner/operators as well as corporate employees could air complaints to an unbiased party. McDonald's put up the resources to ensure that decisions were fair, which over the years was not insignificant, and the ombudsman, interestingly, did not report officially to anyone—and therefore was not influenced in decision making by executive management. The ombudsman heard some cases himself, but in the situations where there was controversy, particularly with issues of impact from new stores being built, he brought an objective operator from another region to work with him on this—a very insightful and fair approach. John Cooke, who served as the first ombudsman, said that during his tenure he fixed about one-third of the cases, after determining that they were not handled properly by the company. In the United States, the program still exists today, with a national ombudsman and a total of three franchise relations ombudsmen—one for each division.

Said former ombudsman Tom Dentice: "The ombudsman system was probably one of the greatest things we did from an integrity standpoint." While not every owner/operator took advantage of the program, those who did seemed to appreciate that the system provided a venue to air grievances. "I think that is one of the programs that absolutely set the foundation of the company having integrity among the franchisee community. Because once the decisions were made, they could appeal to the company president, for example, here in the United States, and the president would sit down and listen to them," Tom added. "I don't think the president ever overturned one." In his tenure as ombudsman, Tom handled very few cases, largely he said because most of the decisions were good ones.

Rick McCoy, a one-time 90-unit franchisee, said the ombudsman program gave owner/operators "someplace to vent." And though some may find fault with the program, it is designed to base decisions on the merits of the case by an unbiased source.

The ombudsman program was also used *prior* to a dispute. On more than one occasion, as the regional manager, I called the ombudsman in when I knew a situation would lead to heavy controversy. Why not get another objective opinion in to make sure the decision is a fair one? It was a real advantage to have that support available to enable me to try to avoid making a poor choice that could have lasting effects.

Owner/operators gave the company high marks for giving them a venue to air concerns. "I think the company makes most of the decisions but listens to the operators and maybe picks up some of it. They think: well, maybe they are right," noted Rick McCoy. "They put together a lot of committees and things that probably did a lot of good for the company."

Lesson Learned

An ombudsman program sends the signal to everyone that the organization strives to be fair in its decision making. It also indicates that the company cares enough to do the right thing and fix what may be broken. It also becomes a great tool to allow staff to vent their concerns and frustrations.

Giving Everyone a Vote

There were other examples of establishing trust and a relationship based on integrity. One example is in voting in the local advertising cooperatives (co-ops) around the country. It was established early on that the McOpCos (company-owned stores) would only have one vote, in all voting matters within the geographic co-ops, no matter how many restaurants it operated. However in many situations, the outcome was heavily influenced by the larger operators who had more votes. The idea was that the company stores could not dominate the voting process and control the co-op. Once again; a system of checks and balances was integrated into the process.

Another example is the ruling that if an operator is disenfranchised by the company, for any reason, the company cannot purchase and operate those restaurants; instead, it will assist in a sale to another franchisee. The concern is that it would be unethical for the parent corporation to have the power to both take away a franchise and then keep it for itself. Although often overlooked, these rather innocuous principles and policies helped to deliver the message of fairness and integrity within the system and its organization.

Honoring Commitments

Company tradition maintained that McDonald's strived to honor verbal communications between the company and suppliers or franchisees. If an officer had made a verbal commitment to someone, even though it was not put down in writing, the company did its best to stand by that commitment. I asked former president Mike Roberts about that. "I remember when people would say, 'This is what the previous regional manager told me,' or, 'This is what the previous zone manager said to me,'" Mike recalled, referring to assurances made to franchisees. "And I would tell them that we are going to try and figure out a way for that to come to life." Mike always made it a point to verify the specifics—clarifying whether a franchisee was promised a specific store versus a new store. And he'd take it from there. "I would say, 'Thank you very much, that's all I needed to hear; we are going to try to make this work.' It was the notion of individuals believing in each other, and that was always the fabric of the company. With company efforts, it inspired trust in the operators, and the people in those roles inspired trust. As the company did well, it translated across the counter."

But that doesn't mean there were not abuses, where trust was questioned. Jim Lewis, a multistore operator in Manhattan, retold a story of how his well-established and successful store felt the impact of a new store opening, which was granted to another operator. As Jim shared with me, he was promised that his largest-volume store would not be negatively affected like that again. Much to his amazement, a number of years later, another new store was being built, threatening to have negative impacts again. And he wasn't being offered the new store! He wondered if leadership had forgotten the conversation; ultimately, though, the issue did eventually get resolved. "The company as a whole had the integrity to fix what needed to be fixed. And it happened through different channels, and over more time than perhaps everyone wanted, but in the end it did get fixed." Jim received compensation for his situation to rectify the loss in revenues in a number of ways, and since that episode, his organization has now grown to a total of 12 stores that he runs. Jim's operations continue to be successful, and the relationship with McDonald's is solid.

During my tenure, I observed that honesty and integrity were demonstrated in some unusual ways. One interesting scenario was the "operator-only" meetings that were held in the corporate offices during the year. The National Operators' Advisory Board (NOAB) had representation from all of the regions around the country. They would meet during the course of the year to hear committee reports and to generally work on various issues that the operators felt were important. While there was much collaboration and communication between the corporation and the

17

members, one feature was the operators-only meeting held each time the group convened. This format enabled operators to feel comfortable talking among themselves, without the pressure or the perceived threat of having any company people attend. It was a great tool for airing out any issues or personality concerns with McDonald's key leadership group. And it worked. There was one unique aspect. In the back of the room, at each session, sat Fred Turner. Fred managed to gain the group's trust, and they allowed him to sit in the back of the room and listen and observe the proceedings. It was a total example of the trust and admiration that Fred embodied for the group. He never spoke, and would only question some of the participants during the break periods for clarity purposes. He understood the unique bond and integrity he was bestowed and had earned by the group and made sure to keep that bond and relationship intact.

18

Food for Thought
How Can You Gain a Group's Trust?

- By your actions and deeds. Walk the talk. Model your own personal integrity.
- By your understanding of your people and their needs and concerns.
- By listening to your staff effectively and intently.
- By following up on your commitments and obligations.
- By giving employees a larger role in decisions within their areas of responsibility. Giving trust will be reciprocated.
- By being ready to defend your subordinates should they be unfairly represented.

Maintaining Integrity with Consumers

When Jim Cantalupo returned from retirement to lead the company as CEO, McDonald's had lost some of its luster. Having acquired Boston Market, Chipotle, and Pret a Manger, McDonald's had taken its eye off the fries, many people felt. Jim brought with him the mission to refocus the company on its core values. To Fred Turner, who was instrumental in bringing him back to the fold, Jim had one directive: "Fix the food." And that meant restoring the food to the quality and standards that had made it a trusted brand with consumers.

It was a moment Jeff Stratton hasn't forgotten. "Fred called a bunch of us together in a conference room," including current CEO Jim Skinner, Jeff told me. "Fred was livid with us, and he was livid because of the small incremental changes that we had made over the past four to five years that ultimately ended up in an unacceptable product, in his opinion, being delivered to the consumer, and he wanted it fixed."

This meeting was held on Friday, October 1, 2003, as Jeff recalled: "Fred said, 'If any of you really care about this, I will be at the Innovation Center tomorrow morning, Saturday morning. If you would like to join me, I am going to go to work on repairing this food, and I would really like your help.' Obviously, we were all there. And it spurred the food team."

This original Food Improvement Team, in true McDonald's style, deployed the three-legged-stool approach: a mix of owner/operators, suppliers, and corporate staff, all the partners—people who cared about the company and maintaining integrity with customers. "We pulled these guys together and we asked them their opinion about the food. And guess what? Their's wasn't much different than Fred's. It started with buns, meat, ingredients, procedures, and, five years later, that food team is as strong and as passionate and as crazed about making our food even better, and we now have teams all over the world."

19

Honesty to Navigate the New York Market

One of the toughest issues that I faced in the region was not only the awarding of a new restaurant to a licensee but also the ensuing arguments over what the sales and rent potentially would be for the new location. There was always a give and take, and the operators knew full well that the rent number—which was based on a formula that included all of the company's expenses for the real estate and construction and development costs were amortized over a number of years— was usually a number that they lived with for the entire 20 years of the agreement. So it was in their best interests to push for the lowest possible rent number. In the New York region, we faced some of the toughest cost structures in the nation, and that challenge only added to the potential for disagreements. I attempted to alleviate this with a simple approach: honesty.

At McDonald's, it was not necessarily common practice to review with licensees the "company's side" of the profit projection, just as they, the franchisees, had to make up their own profit projections as well. But since we encountered many unusual costs, it forced rent percentages to exceed the national averages. This made many of these "one-offs" or one-on-one negotiations. Although our sales were in the top tier of all regions, escalated real estate costs still gave many of the operators concern. By the same token, I had to protect the financial viability of the new development as well. Once again, the issue of balance and fairness was at play.

Working with my team, we reviewed the estimated numbers, showing how the rent was established, and how we arrived at the split for both the operator and the company. We tried to maintain a two-thirds/one-third split of profit (the larger split to the operator), showing them that their investment, while much less, returned them a greater yield. Obviously, that was predicated on assumptions of sales and expenses, some within our control, and some not, but that was the risk of any potential investment. And, of course, there was no guarantee. But they also had the knowledge that if sales were off, adjustments *could be made*, but they had to demonstrate an ability to run an efficient operation. There was a clear quid pro quo. Through honest and open discussion, both sides could understand the other's point of view and make the decisions based on facts and educated assumptions.

Jim Lewis recalled the perspective of his uncle, Dick Lewis, one of the early franchisees in the development of McDonald's in Manhattan. Dick had a lot of experience in negotiating these rents, receiving one of the first "special rent" stores, and at the time, having the highest-rent store in the nation. "He would tell me to always remember that both sides are guided by the business," Jim noted recently. "And it's a business deal first; and what makes it work is each side taking care of their own business needs and it automatically builds balance." Knowing that both the operator and company come to the table with integrity helped achieve that balance.

Trust Bank

Al Golin, chairman of Golin Harris, the public relations team that has served McDonald's since 1957, developed a philosophy called "Trust Bank" that has served the company well. Al described it in a 2005 interview with *Advertising Age* as "building up deposits of goodwill in this bank of trust and to call on it if you ever need it in terms of a crisis. And that was something that McDonald's believed in very thoroughly. McDonald's really set the tone for an industry that [at the time] had a very dubious reputation."

In my tenure at McDonald's, I saw the Trust Bank's influence throughout the corporation, whether it was in philanthropy, supporting a colleague who hit on hard times, or standing by a supplier. I saw it even in many a McDonald's feel-good ad, which, for example, might show an older teenage brother sharing his fries with his preteen sister, much to the delight of her girlfriends. These ads spoke volumes about McDonald's as a trusted friend and a place where families could gather in the community. And, as I explore in much further depth in the remaining chapters, you will see that the Trust Bank, the honesty and integrity of McDonald's, was not just lip service.

In Summary

Honesty and integrity have been the keystone to McDonald's growth. Without it, the organization never would have inspired the trust and confidence that its partners—the vendors and franchisees—put into the company. These traits have spilled over to the customer, who expects a certain experience when she or he walks into any McDonald's unit. And they have spilled over into the community, which expects nothing short of a good corporate citizen from McDonald's. Organizations that do right by their stakeholders can anticipate the same in return. And that's a definite plus when navigating today's challenging business climate—it's always better to have partners that help you put your best foot forward.

Key Learnings

- ✔ Build an organization where stakeholders know they will be treated fairly and respectfully.
- ✔ Choose honesty and integrity over quick profit opportunities to build lasting partnerships that enable key players to grow strong together. Giving trust elicits trust.

✔ Dissolve any relationships that even hint at being unethical, immoral, or illegal.

✔ Keep your eye on the prize: your customers. There is a reason they put their faith in you. Without an organization that espouses honesty and integrity, the quality of service to your customers will suffer.

✔ Be transparent. When people see that you have nothing to hide, they will work with you, not against you. Make your word your commitment. Say what you mean, and do what you say, beyond reproach. Have personal integrity.

✔ Express your role as a good corporate citizen. You will enhance your reputation and touch lives in ways you may have never expected.

✔ Be accountable to your people and your actions. Follow through on your commitments.

Relationships

McDonald's was like a surrogate family.

—Frank Behan, former zone manager and
senior vice president, McDonald's

While relationships matter in all organizations, they are the very basis for the entire system at McDonald's. They run deep from the heart, driving McDonald's forward. "Relationships are everything in business. You cannot function as a highly successful organization without maintaining relationships," said Ed Rensi, a former president and CEO of McDonald's USA.

The Three-Legged Stool

These relationships were the basis of what Fred Turner famously refers to as "the three-legged stool"—a phrase that comes up again and again when McDonald's culture is examined. This term refers to the relationship between the three partners to the system's success: owner/operators, suppliers and corporate staff. Each is dependent on the others to support the group as a whole.

Fred has always believed that the operators, those closest to the customer on a daily basis, are the ones who can best help to feed and nurture the system. And that belief continues to this day.

"The three-legged stool. I loved it. I grabbed it. I ran with it. It said a lot to me," Fred said to me recently. "It highlights the important role of the suppliers. Then you have the company people. But under the company people, you had the employees of the licensee. Managers and supervisors. Company people working with key people with the operator."

Case in point: Chicken McNuggets. What do they have to do with relationships? Plenty, as Ed Rensi reminded me. Especially when you add in a solid dose of strategic leadership.

"Relationships are all about trust, and sometimes when you are dealing with strategic leadership, and Fred used to say this, and I attribute this to him, and it is the single most important characteristic of McDonald's even to this day, that Fred Turner was an unbelievable strategic leader," Ed told me. "And he nurtured his relationships." Ed described the Chicken McNuggets program, of which he was head of product development. Fred asked Ed if he had the right people working on this project, to which Ed replied, "Well, hell, yeah. We have the best people in product development." But Ed realized that he didn't have the best people. Because of Fred's personal relationships with Herb Lotman, a primary meat supplier, and Bud Sweeney, who developed McDonald's Filet-O-Fish, as Ed recalled, "when Fred said 'Go make me Chicken McNuggets,' they holed up in a room, that's all they worked on, and it was because of Fred's relationship with those people. And he said 'Trust me,' and they did." As Ed pointed out, the strategic leader has to say at some point: "Trust me and follow my lead. You may not know exactly how this is all going to work out, but trust me." Ed continued, "Fred was a guy that invested a tremendous amount of trust in people, and therefore people trusted him. He was a man of his word."

Many of these relationships in the early years went way beyond a normal customer-client association. Pat Paterno, a sales manager for a milk company that supplied milk products from 1961 through 1991, told me how his company actually helped a new operator financially. "Fred called me up one time and asked if we could help out a new operator in upstate New York," Pat said. "The guy needed money to open the store. So we lent him the money, and he became a client as well. He paid us back, and everything was fine." Unusual perhaps, but it fostered a pay-it-forward element that's so pervasive in the system. Perhaps that might explain the rest of the story, as Pat reminisced with me about a time years later, when the situation was somewhat reversed. At the time, his employer could not afford to send him to an operator convention. "I mentioned to one of the operators that I don't know what to do. I don't want to say 'I will pay for myself,' I don't want the company to look bad, I don't know how to handle it. I don't think that I am going to go." Sensing his disappointment, the operator made a few phone calls and within a week told Pat the operators were paying for the trip. And they wanted his wife there as well. "I tell ya, tears came to my eyes," recalled Pat. Those were how deep the relationships grew out of mutually working together to help each other.

Vendors put so much faith in McDonald's and its people that they even bailed out the company in 1959 when it was about to lose everything on its first real estate deal gone bad. It seems that construction money was pocketed, leaving contractors unpaid, and resulting in uncompleted stores. As creditors put pressure on McDonald's, the company was faced with the need to raise $500,000 cash in a matter of days (money it didn't have in those early years) or face bankruptcy. "McDonald's was actually out of money and couldn't make payroll," recalled Ted Perlman, a supplier. Ted's father, Lou Perlman, was one of a handful of vendors who pitched in $100,000—a lot of money in the 1950s—

to save McDonald's. Only true believers would rescue a parent company in the fashion of Lou Perlman and the other suppliers, including Continental Coffee, Honey Hill Dairy, Mary Ann Baking, and Interstate Foods. The deep relationship that the company shares with vendors today was in full force in McDonald's initial history.

Peter Grimm, a longtime bun supplier and distributor for McDonald's, had an interesting perspective on the relationship: "At most companies, I am a supplier; but at McDonald's, I am important. Big difference. Vendors to other organizations come and go, vendors aren't partners. We were just a vendor to the other companies we worked with. I have never been in another place where a relationship like this exists."

Got Your Back

One of the recurring comments to come up in many of the interviews with staff and licensees was the notion that support was always there when needed. The entire premise behind franchising is the concept that licensees are in business for themselves, but not by themselves. Mike Roberts, former president of McDonald's, put it this way: "You execute your job and you do it in the highest level you are capable of, and we [the company] have your back covered." Sam Munroe, a 14-store operator in Houston, felt equally supported: "You always feel [that] if you do what has to be done in your store or stores to the best of your ability, you know that you will not be left hanging out alone. The relationships that you develop during that period are the relationships that you will have the rest of your life."

Retired owner/operator Irv Klein believes McDonald's early devotion to franchisees made the system what it is today. "If they had to make a decision, and the decision was what was best for the corporation or what was best for the operators, they came down on the side of the operators," Irv told me. Ray and Fred "did the right thing by the operators. They needed an operator community to have a healthy company. I've always believed that's the key, that's the secret." Owner/operator Sam Samaha agreed. "I always felt comfortable with McDonald's, even though we may have had differences, if you will, as it is in any organization. But a handshake in McDonald's from the time I was there was as good as any legal document," he told me. "I never had a lawyer; never retained a lawyer because I would always use McDonald's legal department. And I think that was the basis for a lot of what we were accomplishing at McDonald's overall," Sam added, referring to the support and confidence he felt was ever present.

Tom Peters explains the franchise relationship in his book, *Thriving on Chaos*: "McDonald's continues to soar. The dealer or franchisee is a cherished member of the family; it's as simple as that. Yet again, few seem to get it."

Fred Turner understood from the very beginning how these solid relationships foster trust, loyalty, and commitment. These qualities permeate throughout the organization, at the lowest levels and up, at times an unspoken ingredient, but still ever present. If you need something, there is that sense that people have your back. Need more buns? Holler, and someone from the crew delivers. Need someone in real estate to conduct a breakeven analysis so you can see if a certain property will work? Call and say, "I need your help right now," and you'll be taken care of, and quickly. Otherwise everyone's productivity will suffer. This teamwork is automatic, at a level of intense support not unlike the kind you see in the military and among emergency workers. Loyalty, support, trust—these are givens. As Paul Schrage, retired senior executive vice president and chief marketing officer, has told me: "Relationships were a part of our business. We became friends. And when the going gets tough, who but your friends would be true?"

29

But trust doesn't come without really knowing a person. For this reason, to this day, Ed Rensi, when interviewing someone in one of his current business ventures, starts the conversation with "tell me about yourself." Inevitably, the person responds by talking about where he or she graduated. "No," Ed likes to tell them. "I want to know about your parents. I want to know about what makes you laugh and what makes you cry." What he wants, Ed said, is to get to the heart of the person's value system. It's the very foundation of trust.

Relationships Based on Service

At McDonald's, add to this Ray Kroc's philosophy of the relationship between the company and operator, where, as stated in Chapter 1, the operator made "the first dollar and the company made the next one," and you have a culture where supporting the operators has long stood as a primary function of the corporate staff. They were our customers. Those of us in the corporation served the operators. You got back to them within 24 hours; you tried your best to accommodate their needs. Frank Behan, former senior vice president and zone manager, called it a "butler mentality." "You love to serve. People make you happy to see that they were satisfied. You have a need to satisfy that person's needs. It's an inner thing, not really learned." All of this has helped to build the vital relationships of the three-legged-stool concept.

"It's basic to who we are and how we do business," Fred pointed out. "It's an owner on premises. They have equity. That's how we're structured."

Relationships between the regions and the corporate office have been another key to the organization's success, and I believe that started with Ray. There are many stories of him calling real estate reps in California and Chicago and asking about a specific site or how a location is doing. In New York, I distinctly remember him in the early 1970s calling an operator on Long Island, who had the distinction of having the lowest-volume store in the northeast. Ray used to call that operator to see how he was doing and encourage him to hang in there and keep driving sales. That close personal relationship was very invigorating to the receiver. The store did eventually do fine with sales and is now a top performer.

Crew, too, rallied to serve the customer. You helped your coworkers so that the product was hot and fresh and came out on time; you pitched in to keep the counter lines short, the restrooms clean.

A Family of Peers and Presidents

And at a most basic level, we were all peers. There was no formality. Ray Kroc was Ray, never Mr. Kroc. And Fred Turner was Fred. As Frank Behan put it: "[It's a] first-name culture—you never called them by their last name. You're equal to me, we're both first name guys. This company's made of 3,000 presidents. Everybody's a president." This means that each franchisee was viewed as an independent president, as were the hundreds of vendors, and in many ways, the regional managers of the corporation running the 28 regions and the operating officers from more than 100 countries worldwide.

As mentioned in John F. Love's *Behind the Arches*, "Care is taken to maintain a family atmosphere by downplaying the corporate hierarchy." It's a philosophy that still resonates on the restaurant floor. As owner/operator Tony Liedtke put it, "When I introduce people, I'll say, 'This is Mary, we work together.' I don't say she is my employee, I don't say, 'She works for me.' *We work together*. It shows respect to them." Building relationships with employees is a key component to successful store operations.

While we had operations spelled out in manuals, many of our calls were from the gut and instinct, based on what we knew

> ## Food for Thought
> How Can You Build Relationships with Colleagues?
>
> Try these ideas:
>
> - Go to lunch with them.
> - Volunteer for a work group within the organization.
> - Send colleagues clippings or e-mails that will interest them.
> - Promote a group activity such as a softball or basketball game outside of the workplace.

worked. There was no textbook theory; remember, most of us grew up in the system and learned our trade on the job, not by attending an MBA program. You can make those judgments when you're working with people you consider family. John Cooke, retired senior vice president, mentioned that in the early years "no major business organization ever left its future in the hands of 19- to 21-year-olds. Many of these same people became successful owner/operators and company executives, starting as crew." They remained with the family, and flourished.

Showing What You're Made Of
In some ways, those entering the company from the academic side may have found themselves at a disadvantage, having to account for the fact that they didn't grow up in the system, as so many of us had. "I had to prove myself," said the director of national training, Kathy May, who runs training at Hamburger University for the United States. Kathy May began working at McDonald's in 1977 at the management level, armed with a college degree, having majored in political science and minored in French and

economics. "You didn't start out as crew," her coworkers would say, adding, "We could tell." What gave Kathy May away was that her procedures were a little too by-the-book; it was obvious that her practices were not handed down. Still, she said, when owners hear that she ran a $3 million restaurant, or that she remembers when Chicken McNuggets were launched, they say, "Now you're okay. It gives you credibility," she pointed out.

You had to have a close relationship with these folks, many of whom were running million-dollar businesses at nights and on weekends, when owners were not present. Ed Rensi noted: "I treated people the way I wanted to be treated. I'd impress them that I knew as much about operations as they did. I'd quote from the operations manual."

And you had to build a foundation where your faith in them was obvious. As Frank Behan recalled: "Ray Kroc believed in you. He always tried to make you reach further than you could grasp. He said, 'I know you can do it.' All you have to do is prove it to yourself. [You tell yourself] maybe I can do it if he thinks I can."

33

And you might even let your guard down, just a little. Frank remembers this conversation with Fred Turner: "One time I said, 'Fred, I feel like I'm cheating the company. I don't know what the hell I'm doing, and I'm getting paid for it.'" As Frank pointed out, it was the bumblebee theory, where the bee doesn't know it can't fly, so it does. Fred Turner, as Frank recalls, turned to him and said, "Guess what? I don't know what the hell I'm doing either, and I'm the president of the company!"

Arguably, they knew what they were doing. Yet they were also immersed in the auspicious endeavor of transferring what they already knew into running and growing what was becoming a very large and complex company. But they had enough faith in each other and in their relationship to kid about their own vulnerabilities. And they each knew they put their trust in very capable hands. We all did, more often than not. This echoed Ray's sentiment: "None of us is as good as all of us."

Food for Thought
How Can You Build Relationships?

Try this interactive exercise, one that I've used to great success and is easily done at any meeting within your group. Ask each person to turn to the individual to the right and provide one example of something he or she appreciates about working with that individual. This exercise never fails to stir some deep positive emotions within the group and get everyone to think of their peers in a new way.

Mentorship

Mentorship played a big part in these relationships. It started at the top and trickled all the way down to crew. Where there are positive relationships, good leaders want what is best for their people. Fred Turner demonstrated this philosophy by mentoring his executive staff to become "McMillionaires," providing a form of wealth management that instructed us how to accumulate stock.

In 1985, Fred handwrote a letter to the McDonald's officers at the time. McDonald's was an $11 billion organization then, and Fred Turner wanted to share his enthusiasm for the potential growth of both the company and its executives in his inimitable manner. This is very characteristic of Fred's style of openness and exuberance at the idea that his staff could become financially secure. Here is that letter:

To Officers McD Corp
The attached list of shares owned as of 12/31/85 is the information made public thru the SEC. As long as your next door neighbor has access to it, you might as well see it.

34

It is my ambition, and I believe a realistic objective, that each of you has an opportunity to become a McMillionaire. Today @ $61/share it would take 16,667 shares to be there. You'll see that 10 have already made it.

Your average holding is 7000 shares. If only half of you were to realize the ambition, the present average is 42% of the way home.

On April 10 of 1987 most of your outstanding options will expire. Just 23 months to go before that clock runs out.

What % of those outstanding options will you end up owning—?
20%?
33%?
50%?
80%?
100%?

Please sit down and try to answer the question—not for me, but for yourself.

When will you exercise—now or later?

You've all got the same obstacles and maze to contend with and work your way there. You're all limited to the same month time frame. You're all leaving the maze at the same time with a number of shares in your hand. Which officer will realize the highest percentage? Which officer will realize the lowest percentage?

I am not trying to establish a contest between you. Notwithstanding, there will be relative winners and relative losers. I am trying to get you to Think.

I am trying to get you to Plan.

I am trying to get you to Realize more Shares.

Hell, I don't know the magic answer. I suppose the best answer is all a matter of timing.

Its interesting—
It's challenging—
These are BIG STAKES.

It's your money.
It's your kids' future inheritance.

Uncle Fred

P.S. After you dope out your maze strategy, please work on
Project II, i.e., how do you double the number of shares you
own as of April 1987? Force yourself to take a piece of paper,
make necessary assumptions, and make calculations, and lay
out a Project II plan. After you finish Project II 92 and Proj-
ect II 97, please wink at me . . . I won't ask what II 97 is. . . .
I just want to know you did the exercise.

Fred

Because most of us had started as crew, from predominately
blue-collar families, we had very little exposure to the path to
becoming prosperous. Our priorities were more about our fledging careers and young families. Many of us had little time or
understanding of such a far-reaching goal of financial security.
And then, out of the blue, we received this handwritten letter that
was sent to our homes. Here was that path to prosperity, handwritten, no less, by Fred Turner, the man responsible for trans-
forming McDonald's into what it is today. Now, as a young,
newly elected officer, I reinvigorated my faith and trust in the
company, feeling much the way I had as an assistant manager
out on a date at a restaurant when I bumped into Pete Hunt, the
franchisee I worked for, who picked up the tab for us—a deep
and meaningful gesture. In both cases, that care, support, and
concern was perhaps the best perk about working within the system. It's a quality that is easily taken for granted when you're in
the system, but something that is sorely missed once you leave.

I never forgot Fred's letter. So, when I had the opportunity, I, in turn, wanted to encourage my staff to think longer term. As a regional manager, I pulled out Fred's letter and reviewed it with my department heads. The essence I wanted to convey to them was still the same: work toward making the company successful, hold on to your options, and keep the stock so that when it is exercised it can have a positive impact on your financial well being. This kind of mentoring was not job related, but a powerful way to nurture staff. Sure, it's the right thing to do. But there's another side to the strategy. Nurture your staff, and you develop the loyalty and trust within the team. Help the staff to work toward financial security, and your workers will become engaged in the goals within the organization and boost their performance. Everybody wins.

When I served as regional manager, I learned a lot from my immediate boss at the time, Rob Doran, the zone manager. Our personalities clicked, and we had a lot in common that nurtured a great friendship as well as business relationship. He immediately came across as genuinely interested in my success and being a true mentor. Besides the everyday support of decisions, he talked about how he, like many of us, started in the stores as crew and was able to move up the organization and what it meant to him, not only professionally but also personally. He spoke about how to manage future family finances. It was yet another sign of how pervasive the notion of wealth management was to the culture of McDonald's. Rob's sincerity and his ability to talk about things so personal as family and finances won me over. He also won over many others and is credited (not often enough) with helping to develop huge numbers of management and executive level staff over his career. And like many McDonald's alumni, he still is active as a consultant and mentor to many within the organization today.

One on One with Mike Quinlan

It's easy for us former McDonald's folks to look back on our tenure nostalgically. And, given McDonald's penchant to "never be satisfied" (see Chapter 3), it's not surprising that some of the best of us look to review our careers with ways to improve the system. Take Mike Quinlan, whose home I visited in a Chicago suburb on a warm winter's day. "If I could go back today," said Mike, referring to changes he would make as CEO, this time around with the gift of hindsight at his side, "I would pick something like a president's counsel, a chairman's counsel, but not as a formal body." This got my interest. "Like a cabinet—but loose?" I asked him. "Maybe individualized," Mike said. "So that there are no politics in the group. And [the group that I set up] would be some company people, some suppliers, a couple of operators [with] whom I would regularly consult, and then aggregate all the input and do what you have to do."

In fact, Mike is serving in that exact capacity at a Wall Street firm, as a mentor to the CEO. "I am able to be of tremendous help to [the CEO] because of the advantage of my experience, and also I have no axe to grind. I've got time, and I don't need to be a director; I like it. And, you know, he can tell me anything and it doesn't go any further. I wish I would have had that; it would have helped me a lot. So that's where I am on relationships, I think that they are very important."

As a consultant today, I agree with Mike that it's critical for leaders to have a confidante who is objective, at arm's distance away, familiar with the business, but not part of the business. These make for the most powerful relationships.

Food for Thought
What Is a Mentor?

Merriam-Webster defines the term as "a trusted counselor or guide." But a true mentor is someone people want to be around. A true mentor inspires the troops to deliver more than they thought possible. Ray Kroc was that kind of leader.

"He was definitely a mentor to me," Fred Turner told me. "I admired him. I loved him. He was a leader and an outstanding person. He set the tone and then would get into personal things. He was interested in people, a genuine interest in people. He loved to tell stories, jokes."

Noted Mike Quinlan, former CEO: "Ray had the ability to take us regular folks and motivate us from being average people to outstanding performers. That is a talent. He had the ability to take us and inculcate us in his dream and have us become not the 12 Apostles, the 100 Apostles." With Mike, the father figure applied in many ways, he said. "He told me a couple of times, after some down time, in many ways he wished he would have a son like me. And it moved me to tears a couple of times. . . . I knew what his ideal was, and I agreed with that ideal and I wanted to be the best in his eyes, because I knew that was the best thing."

A Hamburger University Welcome

At Hamburger University (HU), many of the restaurant managers who attend classes "have never been on an airplane before and never been out of their hometown," Kathy May noted. They fly into Chicago, and are picked up by limo, and driven to the Hyatt Lodge at McDonald's Campus. The walls of the Lodge are adorned with eye-catching paintings, and the grounds and interior are dotted with aesthetic sculptures. "There is crystal at the table, leather chairs, beautiful carpet," Ed Rensi pointed out. That décor makes the statement that "we respect our store managers," he added.

Inside HU, there is a bright yellow-and-orange larger-than-life statue of Ronald McDonald, sitting on a bench. The students sit alongside Ronald, snapping photos, Kathy May said. During the course of the training, an officer of the company addresses them. The entire HU curriculum is worth 42 college credits, and courses are taught in 28 languages, to support a diverse culture and accommodate its global workforce (though there are six other HUs around the world). And to make this global workforce feel welcome, HU displays the flags that represent the countries of the visitors that are there that week, and those that work on the premises. This is another way the company shows the importance of relationships, in recognizing our global organization and the diversity of the folks who walk into the university.

Vendor Relationships

Vendors have played a big role in the three-legged stool. Just ask Ted Perlman, whose father, Lou Perlman, started Martin-Brower, McDonald's largest distributor.

"McDonald's is probably one, if not the only, company where the word *relationships* has real meaning," Ted told me. "Some people complain that it's not the same today as it was yesteryear; however, my comment on that is the world and the marketplace has changed."

But in recalling McDonald's early history, Ted said, "The relationship was born because McDonald's was a personality-driven company, not a structure-driven company, and when you go back to Ray and Fred, you talk about passion, you talk about immediacy, all this can only happen when you have people-to-people dependency."

And, through that dependency, trust was born—the kind of trust that gets recognized throughout the system. Ted pointed out that "right from the beginning it started with Ray, but Fred embodied the idea that if it's not good for the units, the stores, it's not good for the corporation, the system, or the public. That, again, is why he created such loyalty from the operators. When Fred was wrong, they forgave him; they knew he was trying to do something in his own mind that was right for the operator." Though Ted speaks of the relationship between the company and the operator, it was really the system that benefited as a whole, with trust as the backbone that inspired confidence in all three components of the three-legged stool.

41

These relationships are a phenomenon that many of us agree is unique to McDonald's. "Here's the reason why you can't develop relationships in most companies, especially with suppliers," Ted said. "How many of these people have people in the same positions, growing up in the organization during the course of 15, 20, 25, 30, 35 years? It doesn't happen in the real world." Ted's comment on employee retention provides another example of the depth of the bench of talent that is constantly developed within the organization. Few staff actually leave, allowing years of development for key managers as they move up the career ladder.

And by and large, Ted added, corporate "understood how to get people's confidence, and they knew if there was a problem somehow [they'd] make it right."

Friends at Work

Many in leadership positions feel you cannot have friendships and still be a boss to an individual. But I have never subscribed to that theory, and most of the folks I have met in my years with McDonald's don't either. When you have true friends in business, they will at times offer constructive criticism, with complete, and sometimes bristling, candor. In such relationships, there is give and take, and you might be surprised how much you can learn, especially from your subordinates. But you must be ready to listen. It's a skill worth honing.

In their book, *First, Break All the Rules,* authors Marcus Buckingham and Curt Coffman analyze the in-depth interviews they conducted with more than 80,000 managers in 400-plus companies. Their conclusions about relations are very revealing:

> *The most effective managers say yes, you should build personal relationships with your people, and no, familiarity does not breed contempt. This does not mean that you should necessarily become best friends with those who report to you—although if that is your style, and if you keep them focused on performance outcomes, there is nothing wrong with doing so. The same applies to socializing with your people—if that is not your style, don't do it. If it is your style, then there is nothing damaging about having dinner or a drink with them, as long as you still evaluate them on performance outcomes.*

The system within McDonald's demanded that friendships were based on more than simply getting along with another person. Perhaps that's why the relationships I formed at McDonald's have persevered, even eight years after I left the system. In an effort to continue these relationships with the alumni of

McDonald's, Fred Turner himself has started a quest to build an organization of those who "subscribe to Ray Kroc's philosophy." The Evergreens (the alumni organization of McDonald's retirees), or McVets, those employees with 20 or more years, stems from a comment made by Ray Kroc, who famously said, "As long as you're green, you're growing." The mission is simply "to maintain contact with McDonald's friends and associates, keep up on McDonald's news and developments, support and preserve the brand, share memories and history with one another and the Company through the Golden Archives, and help sustain McDonald's heritage of 'giving back' through community involvement and charitable activities."

At the Worldwide Convention in April 2008, more than 13,000 McDonald's licensees, vendors, and company people gathered to celebrate, learn, and reach for the opportunities that the business climate has for them. And starting a day before the convention, the McVets and Evergreens were more than 2,000 strong to welcome the current three-legged team and wish them success in their respective journey.

Jim Collins, in his book, *Good to Great*, writes: "Members of the good to great teams tended to become and remain friends for life. In many cases, they are still in close contact years or decades after working together. These people had fun!"

In my mission to decipher just what those McDonald's relationships were made of, I spoke to former McDonald's CEO Mike Quinlan. "You need to have relationships with people who know enough to give you usable input," said Mike. "Realistic input, honest input from people who have no axe to grind and who respect you for everything you are, the good, the bad, the package that you offer them. But you really need someone who can talk to you about the business both personal and professional. And give you food for thought." Yet, as Mike pointed out, what you do with that information is up to you.

A Line in the Sand

I spoke with Claire Babrowski, former senior executive vice president and chief restaurant operations officer at McDonald's, who now serves as chief operations officer at Toys "R" Us. "You know that management was looking for trust and respect," she told me. Claire was referring to a line in the sand; it wasn't enough to like someone, you needed each other's frankness.

That was the case when I served as a training manager in the early 1970s. At the time, my team conducted training "road shows" throughout the region, and we were constantly tweaking to get them right. We measured our success by giving our trainees surveys in which they provided feedback on the content, presentation, and quality of our programs. We reveled in those sessions. Over dinner, we read the feedback aloud, particularly if it was very good—or not so good, giving us all a reason to jab the poorly reviewed consultant. While it was all good-natured and fun, and many a beer was spilled laughing or chiding someone, these sessions had a purpose. They set the standard for our product. It got so that even a slight comment that was not positive was met with introspection and, of course, pressure on the consultant who was responsible. Yet I may have set the bar too high.

One night, after dinner, I was left with one consultant, the most senior of them all. Danny was a great consultant. About six years older than most of us, putting him at early thirties at the time, he had served at other corporations besides McDonald's, although he had been with the company for the last five years. Danny took the daily stresses in stride, and because of his wonderful personality, he was a hit with the operators and staff. He was a wonderful counterbalance to our high-energy, high-pressure group. A fixture at all after-hours socializing, he became one of the unofficial leaders within the entire region, and provided the glue that kept the staff together. All organizations usually have someone like this, and they contribute to the morale and well-being of the group in ways many of us never get an opportunity to observe or realize.

On this particular evening, Danny asked if I had a few minutes to spare. When I said yes, he proceeded to say that he was concerned for the group. He felt I might be pushing the team too hard and it was starting to hurt morale. They worked harder than many of the others in operations, putting in longer hours and on weekends, and it was beginning to show; they were weary, they complained—but I seemed oblivious to it. My quick defensiveness made me remind him that "we" won accolades from corporate for our department. While he agreed, he felt I should pull back a bit and we would still be okay.

As I reflected back on his comments on the drive back home, I began to see the poignancy in Danny's words. I was grateful to know this truth, and yet I was still hurt that I let the team down and that they actually felt that I pushed too hard. Still, I wondered why the other consultants hadn't spoken up. I thought we were closer than that. Yet, as Mike Quinlan alluded to me in a recent interview, it was up to me to decide what to do with Danny's comments. As Danny's insights resonated deep down, and I realized that he was right and I was wrong, I made a conscious effort to ease up and increase the appreciation and recognition of the group. While that tactic worked, and everything was better subsequently, it left a big impression on me.

Danny's frankness was a direct product of the system. There was an openness of dialog, and a sense that, regardless of titles, we were on equal footing. Sure, as a person within the organization you might get your head chopped off for speaking up, but the underlying culture at McDonald's was all about speaking your mind with openness, candor, and facts. Danny was the kind of friend who spoke the truth, and I quickly appreciated his perspective.

45

Still, I hated the thought that had been festering for some time, and I could have corrected myself much earlier. I made a commitment to cultivate a better network of feedback from people in whom I could confide, people with whom I could raise questions, discuss issues, and seek advice. One group that I nurtured over the years was my administrative assistants, all of them very capable and valuable. Their influence, advice, and counsel were incredibly helpful. They helped me to look far better than I was.

Good relationships will allow others not only to approach you with insights but also to challenge your thinking. Fred Turner had specific thoughts on this: "People that go along with what I want, all of the time, I become suspicious of them. . . . It isn't always fun to have your boat rocked, but when people would say 'it's a mistake,' there's a positive way to say it. It was a way to make a point."

46

People to Lean On

As Dave Natysin, retired corporate vice president in charge of company operations for the East, put in a memo to "The McFamily" in 2007: "At McDonald's it's always been about being up close and personal. That's the secret sauce in people development that others just can't seem to grasp when they research McDonald's." And as I can attest, people development springs from all sides—your superiors, your peers, and even your own direct reports. It's how we get better, or as Dave, in his memo, expressed, McDonald's leadership has the "willingness and ability to listen to everyone, from the newest Crew person to the Chairperson, from our customers to our critics, from those that complement our restaurants to those that criticize our restaurants."

In listening and learning, we found people to lean on, a trait that is inherent within the system. Ray Kroc had Fred Turner as his backup. And Fred turned to Mike Quinlan and Jim Cantalupo, both of whom would later serve as chairman and CEO.

Ed Rensi expressed it this way: "Everything I learned, I learned from somebody else." And he looked at his people holistically. "I was tolerant of someone's buckets of weaknesses as long as I could maximize on their strengths."

In finding my own backup, I sought those with the ability to hit me with the tough criticism that I needed to do my job well. As Fred put it: "If we all agree all of the time, one of us is unnecessary." But I had to do my part too, and put my own ego aside so I could really listen and understand their perspective. Fred describes this as "having your ears on," and he's right. You have to be a deep listener.

Lesson Learned

Seek out and develop a network of individuals who you can rely on for good feedback and advice. Don't react, don't be defensive . . . listen.

Be in the present.

Jesters and Conflicts

That's not to say that the organization didn't have its share of "court jesters" who rallied around a leader, buttered up the boss, and harped on all that was favorable to earn their place in his or her eyes. I think that most of us can relate to someone in an organization who exhibits these behaviors, which often result in jealousies, ill will, and a waste of time and energy. Such behavior goes on in most organizations, and it's something that management should be aware of. As Mike Quinlan put it, "You have to be careful though that you don't develop pets."

To me, it was troubling at times how often leadership did not see these situations for what they really were and the negative morale that developed when this was allowed to happen. Like other organizations, McDonald's has at times fallen victim of that culture in its history, a scenario Mike describes as "very anti-success, very anti–the culture of our company. So you have to guard against that, and that's the CEO's job to guard against that. And it's easy to say now, looking back, it's easy to say things later, but the leader has to set that culture up."

Like other organizations, some of the conflicts within McDonald's have bred contempt that sadly has lingered on for years. Yet as upset as any of these individuals may still feel today, the system has proven strong enough to withstand any hard feelings. Clearly, many of the big successes were the result of the honest feedback that was encouraged where the relationships were nurtured. The company was the better for it, and in typical McDonald's style, the person providing that feedback received some deserving accolade.

48

2 + 2+ 2 = 12: Synergy

Relationships within the McFamily have long been based largely on the shared motivation to succeed. Succeed and you prosper, big time. "The McFamily is bigger than any one part," Mike Quinlan told me. "It is a great example of 2 + 2 + 2 = 12. Not six, 12. The intelligent, mature, unselfish members of the McFamily truly recognize that, with McDonald's, 2 + 2 + 2 = 12. You mess up the 2 + 2 + 2, and the 12 disappears." As Mike pointed out, this requires integrity across the board, though as in any family, there is always a black sheep or two whose motivation and dedication isn't aligned with everyone else's: "The 2 + 2 + 2 = 12 depends upon each of us being willing to be mostly unselfish and to sacrifice our personal good for the greater good of the McFamily. If that breaks down, you're in trouble. We have been able to keep that together pretty well all of these years through a combination of many factors: luck, expertise, timing, intimidation, excellence in execution, inspired leadership, and the chance for gain, the risk–reward thing has always been there. I don't know which part of it is most important. There probably isn't any one thing that is most important, but what we have done is amalgamated a universe of people that, even subconsciously, live by the 2 + 2 + 2 = 12."

Lesson Learned

Mike's "2 + 2 + 2 = 12" is sometimes referred to as "partnering," where two or more individuals achieve actions that each is incapable of by themselves. Partnering has a number of distinct advantages:

- Fostering the synergy to brainstorm and share ideas.
- Leveraging each other's strengths, providing insights to a variety of diverse thoughts.
- Compensating for weakness. Some team members may not be able to see the big picture; others may not be good at evaluating long-term effects. By partnering, we can offset each others' weaknesses.
- Assisting in selecting best policies. By partnering, we can examine the pros and cons of policies and see different points of view.

49

A Showdown

Of course, it would be naïve to believe that honest relationships were always in full force, constantly driving the company forward. There were times, of course, when the company stumbled, when operators made mistakes. Take, for instance, the debacle the company faced in 1975 with the McDonald's Operators Association (MOA), whose members, all of them franchisees, challenged the company. This was a rogue organization intent on a revolt. The MOA demanded the right to renew their franchise automatically when the agreement expired, the influence to prevent new franchisees from entering the system (eliminating future competition), and the ability to loosen the standards the system held on its operators. This rocked the very foundation of the company's success, and it threatened the relationship that had served the system so well. But it also proved a weakness: the organizational structure lacked the checks and balances needed to keep the system healthy and fair to all sides. This became the linchpin in the importance of building those much-needed checks and balances by allowing operators a forum to express themselves and seeking to gain a collaborative approach toward working with the franchisees. Ultimately, McDonald's turned the situation around by forming the National Operators' Advisory Board, whose members were elected by the operators within each region and have a national forum for debate and conversation. Once again, this was a unique solution, at the time, that allowed the partnership to prosper.

Being There When It Really Counts

I began to cultivate relationships from my early days on the restaurant floor. As crew, we challenged one another to be the best. "Can you handle it?" we asked with bravado, basically implying: "Are you good enough at your station to keep up with the crowds and not let the rest of the team down?" We called out "I got it!" providing meaningful assurance that we wouldn't run out of fries or slow down at the grill; otherwise, as we all knew, if one of us screwed up, we'd all feel the impact, and quickly. This was in the spirit of camaraderie. I remember one Christmas coming home with an armful of presents from my fellow workers, much to the surprise of my parents, who never expected I'd encounter such a culture at a job flipping burgers, as Dad liked to remind me. But I wasn't surprised. Our relationships ran deep, and my coworkers and I actually had a deeply felt respect and admiration for each other. And besides, we truly enjoyed working together.

Yet relationships went deeper than spreading happy cheer at Christmas. Take Kathy May. Kathy recalled working in New York City and, while out on the road with a manager, getting into a car accident in the company car on the East River Drive: "My [human resources] manager came from Long Island and sat in the waiting room at Bellevue Hospital for five or six hours to drive me back. She picked me up the next day. We're very much family, you just do that."

Kathy has that same sense in the Oak Brook, Illinois, home office, where a lot of the workers are transplants who are miles away from their blood relatives. "I have someone out on short-term disability," she said. "Every other week we chip in for a cleaning service for her because she's not supposed to do any heavy lifting." And then, echoing the spirit of Ray Kroc, who believed in the power of what people can accomplish together, she added, "None of us can afford it. But all of us can afford it."

Food for Thought
How Can You Determine Which Relationships in Business Are Good Ones?

In working with leadership classes, I like to share this question, which I think perfectly sums up the essence of a good relationship . . . and that is to ask myself, "Do I learn from and enjoy being around this person?" I think it's the simplest form of evaluation. And, of course, it makes you reciprocate and look at yourself through others' eyes . . . do I make it enjoyable for people to be around me?

Lesson Learned

Companies, organizations, and the workplace are social units. The ability to create a culture of mutual respect and enjoyment within the environment of the organization can only enhance the overall success of the group.

Relationship Power

One of the basic tenets of managing people came fairly quickly in my short time working in the store. I was "in charge" of the floor at the time, sometimes referred to as a "swing manager," someone who "swung" from shift to shift between the night manager and the general manager who worked during the day. While I was barely older than most of the crew, and many of us had been friends for a while, I saw the need to balance a position of authority (commonly referred to as *position power*) within the ranks if I was going to manage effectively. But I also needed to earn the *relationship power*, one that is gained by acquiring the trust and respect of the group. It was a delicate balancing game for any young manager.

On this particular day I entered the back-room area, where I'd posted on a bulletin board the next week's schedule. A crowd had gathered, and as I moved toward them, I overheard one individual mouthing off about the "stupid managers" and the "unfair schedule," threatening to quit if it weren't fixed. He was actually one of our better workers, and a friend of mine to boot. Just as the group noticed I was there, he proceeded to rip the schedule off the board and toss it into the wastebasket nearby.

This now became one of those moments when the entire group uniformly waited for my response to this act of anger. I needed to do "the right thing," which instinctively I realized would produce a response that would trigger long-term ramifications beyond this incident. With sheer spontaneity, I mustered up all the maturity and professionalism I could, telling him to "punch out and come in tomorrow to discuss your job." It proved to be the right call. It showed the rest of the crew that I meant business and that, whether friends with this person or not, would not tolerate behaviors like that. And it provided some slack, as postponing the conversation to the next day allowed us both a cooling-off time, as well as gave an opportunity for senior management to collaborate on the right approach, effectively taking the responsibility off me to determine his fate. The crew now viewed me in a different light, and my requests were met with a much quicker response than previously. And this crew person and I remained friends; he later admitted he was wrong and apologized. So, you can manage relationships on the job if you just keep the perspective. It's what the system was all about—friendship, but with established behavioral norms that set the tone of acceptable conduct, as parameters set in any family.

Lesson Learned

Don't be afraid to develop relationships on the job, even as a boss. They are vital and important in establishing the environment you want to create. Keep in mind to balance the importance of the work expectations and behaviors, and that regardless, no exceptions are made. In the end it is about business, but that does not preclude enjoying those friendships. True friends will understand not to cross the line.

Deep Ties to Our Customers

As important as our relationships to our colleagues and our vendors are, our strongest commitment is to our customers, whether it's the company's tie to owner/operators, discussed earlier in the chapter, or the system's devotion to the customer, both in the store and in the community at large.

Commitment to the community is evidenced by McDonald's corporate responsibility, perhaps most obvious in the Ronald McDonald House Charities, whose proceeds support "homes away from home" for families with seriously ill children receiving treatment at nearby hospitals and providing 6,000 beds for families worldwide every night. Employees, owner/operators, suppliers, and even customers raised more than $60 million for Ronald McDonald House Charities in 2005.

Ed Rensi commented to me on his personal involvement in establishing the first Ronald McDonald House in Philadelphia: "I didn't do the Ronald McDonald House because I thought it was good for me. I did it because my heart cried for [Philadelphia Eagles tight end] Fred Hill and Fran Hill. My heart cried for them because their baby, their little three-year-old girl, had leukemia and they didn't know what to do. And I had some great people around me who said, "We can make this work,' and I said, 'Okay, let's make it work.'"

"Making it work" seems to be a prevailing theme on many levels of the system when it comes to giving back. For example, while McDonald's Corporation kicked in $5 million to Hurricane Katrina victims, Kathy May said employees personally raised $75,000, and helped managers and crew find homes.

And that's just one example—others include feeding emergency workers at Ground Zero and after the crash of TWA Flight 800 in Center Moriches, New York. Kathy described these efforts as yet another instance of employees rallying to help another, the way she and her colleagues raised money for their coworker out on disability. "There's the sense that people take care of you," she said. "And the public sees the end result."

Lesson Learned

Part of Ray's original mission was to give back to the community, which he understood was good for sales and public relations. He encouraged everyone in the system, as it got bigger, to give back at a higher level. Today, McDonald's highlights its charitable givings at employee conventions, on its Web site, in its Corporate Responsibility Report, in brochures, and elsewhere. Organizations large and small can showcase their community support in the same way. This approach helps strengthen an organization's bond with employees and vendors as well as the public. It also sends a clear message as to what the organization represents.

One on One with Ed Rensi

Ed and I met for breakfast one morning at the Hyatt Lodge at McDonald's Campus. He shared his thoughts about not just leadership principles at McDonald's but also the mentors and friends that one gathers "growing up" in the system. "I have a tremendous amount of internal satisfaction," Ed told me. "I miss the people terribly. Everything that I am about today is because of what I learned at McDonald's. I have no way of thanking the McDonald's system ever."

Ed's sentiments validated what I've been thinking all along about my own experience. In particular he expressed the profound sense of loyalty I, too, feel about people who take the time and interest in helping you achieve.

As Ed put it: "I would do anything in the world for Fred Turner. Anything. Because he took a schoolteacher from Ohio and allowed me to know and explore things that I would have never known or explored."

Not for Everyone

Did everyone buy into the McFamily? No, not everyone. A lot of that sense of family boiled down to shared values, and if you didn't share those values, than you no doubt were not a good fit at McDonald's. One staff member at the Oak Brook campus office distinctly recalled a new employee who after a couple of days on the job stood up at noon, and proclaimed, "You are all nuts!" and never returned. Others who couldn't give their all to McDonald's core values—about the customer experience, the commitment to talent, honoring business ethics, giving back to our community, growing the business profitably, striving to improve, and believing in the three-legged stool as the premise of the McDonald's system—either were asked to go or left on their own.

Sometimes the relationships between corporate and franchisee get strained, which may seem like somewhat of a contradiction. "We are so helpful to franchisees, so understanding and caring," one Oak Brook executive said. "But it flips when we have to be the standards enforcer."

Every family has its own set of issues where someone feels slighted or another is angered. Like other families, some hard feelings still remain. Despite that, no ex-employee I spoke with had a bad word to say about McDonald's, which was obvious to me when I met 2,000 other McVets and Evergreens at the 2008 Worldwide Convention. Even those who had been let go, or laid off in a restructure, still showed a passion for the system. They may have harbored resentment or frustration with a particular individual, but they still seemed to relish the time spent within the system, as a rule. You would be hard pressed to find anyone within the McFamily who doesn't value the system and the foundation of those relationships between owner/operators, suppliers, and company employees.

In Summary

At McDonald's, relationships run deep. From crew to CEO, from vendor to licensee, we were and are all in the system together. We turn to one another for support and insights, and know that backup is always there. People can excel much more than they ever imagined if they know they have the encouragement and reinforcement of others who believe in them.

Key Learnings

✔ Determine who in your organization makes up the three-legged stool—the key stakeholders—and find ways to nurture those partnerships to best achieve your company's goals. Remember, trust is essential in a relationship.

✔ Find the time to really get to know the people with whom you work. Learn about their motivations and their passions so that you best know how to incorporate and develop their talents. Take an interest.

✔ Don't be afraid to befriend those with whom you work closely, but base those friendships on establishing trust and working cooperatively toward the organization's goals.

✔ Build a team culture, a "we" versus "I," where colleagues know they can count on one another so that if someone falters there is always someone there to keep the momentum.

✔ Mentor your people so that they can thrive, not only professionally, but financially, by addressing quality-of-life issues.

3

Standards:
Never Be Satisfied

The quality of a leader is reflected in the standards they set for themselves.

—Ray Kroc

Those of us with ketchup in our blood, the ones who rose through the ranks and were turned on in a competitive way, had a saying: *never be satisfied*. And we weren't. This statement spoke volumes about McDonald's culture. We were always looking to beat yesterday's sales, cut energy expenses, increase our customer counts, and lower costs to the stores. We were driven to be faster, cleaner, and better. The best of us were always on the lookout to exceed expectations.

Ray knew from the very beginning that high standards would set the company apart, as he told the McDonald brothers on Dictaphone tapes from the late 1950s: "Our policies, our sound way of doing things, is paying off. And we have the respect of top-notch people. I now know of four 15-cent hamburger deals being Henry's, Carroll's, Chef Burger, and Golden Point. And heaven knows how many more there will be. And they are going to be run loose as a goose. Those fellows are going to do any doggone thing they want to do, and the owners of the name are just going to let them do anything they want to as long as they are getting money out of it. It will be survival of the fittest. And I am just as sure as I am sure that I am dictating this sleeve that we are going to be at the top of the list of the fittest."

McDonald's has always been a results-oriented company. "We were continuously looking for a better way to do things, and then a revised better way to do things, and then a revised, revised better way," Fred Turner is quoted as saying in *McDonald's: Behind the Arches*, written by John F. Love.

So it went without saying that company executives sought nothing but the best. Golden Arches lore has it that Ray Kroc once closed down an underperforming restaurant that was dirty, under-staffed, and poorly run. That information was finally verified to me by Tom Dentice, retired executive vice president: "Ray pulled into the lot, and the lines were all the way out to the flagpoles." As the story goes, Ray jumped up on one of the outdoor tables and said to everyone, "I'm Ray Kroc, I own McDonald's, and this restaurant doesn't meet our standards: It's terrible and I'm embarrassed, so I'm closing the store." Nobody would dispute the sentiment behind the tale: substandard was unacceptable, and that has always been the case. Fred Turner remembers one store in Florida in particular: "They were a mess. Everything was screwed up. Ray had a fit. Kicked the metal door closed. He went out and slammed it with his foot. He was so mad he couldn't see straight. Everything was wrong. He couldn't live with it."

One story about Ray's legendary standards was told to me by Ed Rensi, retired president of McDonald's. Ed recalls touring stores with Ray Kroc: "We go into the first store. Ray walks up to the counter and gets a cheeseburger, a small fries, and a strawberry milkshake. We go sit down, and I am eating—I think I had gotten a bag of fries. So we are eating and eating, and he says to me, 'Ed, I want you to go over there and take all the food in the bin and throw it out. This food is awful.' I said, 'okay,' and he goes, 'no, I'll do it.' He walks over and asks to see the store manager. The store manager comes out, and [Ray] says, 'I am Ray Kroc, and I want you to take down all the prices on the menu board.' The manager says, 'Why?' And [Ray] says, 'Because your food is not worth anything. It doesn't taste good, it's dry, old.' So the manager starts taking the plastic pricing pieces out. And I say to Ray, 'What did you tell him?' He said, 'Ed, are you proud of this food?' I said, 'No, not at all.' He said, 'Well, why didn't you do something about it?' He said, 'I did something. Never walk by a problem. Fix it.'"

And all of us lived by those words. Don Horowitz, retired executive vice president and chief legal counsel, told me of an incident early in his career when he and his wife, Judy, happened to be headed toward a reception when they stopped into a McDonald's on the way. The front lawn was full of litter. The two of them began picking up the garbage, even though they were both dressed for a formal event. "The manager never did know who those two well-dressed folks were that decided to clean his front lawn," Don laughingly recalled. I wonder how many corporate attorneys would have emulated Don's approach to such a situation.

Those who rose within the system believed in the same philosophy as Don, and that's no surprise, as it was engrained in the system from day one. "Ray set high standards even before he could afford them, and I respected him for that," says Frank Behan, a former zone manager.

Many of those standards had the ability to become an indelible print on our values. Willis Smart, former regional vice president and now an operations vice president with Dunkin Brands, told me with vivid recollection his experience with McDonald's emphasis on standards. "On my first trip to the corporate office, I was maybe 23 at the time . . . I remember walking into the Plaza building [at the Oak Brook home office], and I hadn't been through the building before. We were walking to the elevator, and I absolutely never forget, there was this guy on his hands and knees scrubbing the thresholds of the elevator, which were either gold or polished brass. I never forgot that. I get goose bumps even now, thinking about how hard we worked to run an A-store, and we were doing it because it was just the way we were raised in the company."

And Willis wasn't alone. Bob Weissmueller, a retired vice president and former CEO of Fazoli's, said, "I always felt, from the day I started, this 'fanatical attention to detail.' The attention to details, to take care of the consumer every day, every time to focus on the customer." Adds former division president Debra Koenig: "McDonald's is pretty strong about making sure that the brand promise was intact in every experience."

From Crew to Corporate

McDonald's sets standards for every task, from crew to corporate. The operations manual clarifies job descriptions and roles, and there are any number of corresponding tools to support each individual, from training videos, to courses at Hamburger University, to field visits, to coaching, and more. These standards included "core competencies" for company staff employees. Interestingly, among the list are "communicating effectively, continuous learning, customer focus, drives to excel, holds self and others accountable, and teamwork and collaboration."

There may have been no better example of setting the standards, than the "Full Field Report" that was used over the years to ensure that quality standards are met in the stores. While the report is now called a "Full Operating Report," its function is the same. The field representative would spend up to two days on an announced visit to the restaurant with the full management team as well as the operator present. Interestingly, both the corporation and the operator learned and developed along with the process. This helped to develop a field staff of seasoned and professional consultants who were, and still are, the envy of restaurant organizations throughout the world, with more than 950 field consultants worldwide currently. That clearly suggests the importance of maintaining standards to the system to this day.

We reviewed and critiqued every aspect of the restaurant and established grades for quality, service, and cleanliness, or QSC, to determine how well the restaurant was operating. This process was a powerful tool that took the QSC standards out of a textbook and clearly defined them within the practicality of the store environment. It did much more than simply establish a grade for a particular location. It forced the field representative to spend quality time in the restaurant, discussing operations and consulting with the key stakeholders within that organization. In reflection, the process helped all parties to grow. In most cases, this interaction built a collaborative goal toward operational excellence and collective pride. It forced the field representative to be well versed in all of the operational details, and allowed him or her to pass on this information to the people that mattered. It taught us how to communicate with these traditionally older and more experienced operators, and forced us to learn the dynamics of communication and the art of consulting. It also had the effect of demonstrating just how well the restaurant could run, effectively setting the bar, as the franchisee would always put the best foot forward during the visit. The best consultants used this as a benchmark for how the restaurant should run all the time. And, a good field visit had its reward, namely the collective rating for achievement of excellence. A high store rating was greatly sought after and coveted by all operators, serving as an indicator for qualifying for possible future store growth. Negative ratings had the opposite effect, suggesting the possible beginning of a process for serious action by the corporation.

There were other consequences as well. As Jim Lewis, a franchisee, mentioned: "If an operator went to a franchisee meeting and you wanted to speak to the group on the floor, if you were not a good operator, then you had no relevance and no credence, nothing, no credibility with the group."

Although a QSC visit was announced to the entire crew of the location, the anticipation, and desire to be the best, was huge. It demonstrated vividly to us the power of getting a team focused. Never underestimate the competitive spirit that is ignited within a team when challenged! As John Cooke, a retired McDonald's senior vice president, mentioned: "A by-product of the full field process was that it identified those who run A-store operations. This is the top performer, and the company promotes these individuals as a standard of excellence for all owner/operators to meet."

We learned to be creative with the results of grading. Instead of just harping on those operators who struggled to get their stores higher ratings in QSC, we also worked it from another angle: *profits*. The company conducted an exhaustive analysis at one point and discovered that for each letter grade improvement in operational levels that a store achieves, it increases annual sales by an average of more than $100,000. This finding got the operators' attention. Now we had an incentive that was fact based, and one that many could grasp: run a better operation and more customers will come. That's pretty basic, but putting measurement behind QSC gave it an understanding that was universal in its appeal to all. Selling the importance of QSC became much easier. And the momentum that drove us to constantly improve never stopped. As Ray Kroc once said, "Whatever we are doing today, we can do better tomorrow." And we took those words to heart.

In the book *The Wisdom of Teams*, authors Jon Katzenbach and Douglas Smith state: "A demanding performance challenge tends to create a team. The hunger to succeed builds unity far better than special incentives or team-building exercises." At McDonald's we had that hunger—a quality that seems to spur the organization on, even today, as it navigates new economic challenges around the world.

One on One with Current CEO Jim Skinner

I asked Jim Skinner about how McDonald's continues to raise the bar. Here's what he shared: "Right now, we need to do a better job on drive-thru capacity and efficiency; it's a huge opportunity. We are still operating on the same kind of drive-thru concept that we had for 30 years. If you look around the world, that is where their big opportunities are—these drive-thrus. The percentages aren't as high, they have fewer of them, but those that have them haven't focused as much on them." Jim looks for opportunities as a way of seeking continuous improvement. As he put it: "It's another way of saying that we are never satisfied."

Lesson Learned

Getting a team focused and engaged on a specific objective that is clearly measurable can provide ownership of achievement and empowerment for the team.

In speaking with Claire Babrowski, a former executive vice president of McDonald's and now COO of Toys "R" Us, she mentioned the culture of "customer obsession." She went on to say that "McDonald's has always seen the store as their real business" and commented how unique that was in many retail organizations and it is a "substantial difference in psyche" to the system. The way the stores operated, their attention to detail, the standards that were established and expected on the store level was that important. It's no wonder that field inspections were such an important part of maintaining high standards.

Food for Thought
Can Your Organization, Business Unit, or Operation Raise Its Standards?

Challenge yourself and your team with these simple questions:

- Do my employees understand what the expectations of the job are?
- How do we define excellence? How is it measured?
- Is success celebrated in my organization? What are the rewards and incentives?
- Is there a constant drive toward improvement? (It's okay to move the goalpost, as long as you take the time to celebrate the previous achievement.)

Importance of Measurement
In researching and writing *First, Break All the Rules*, authors Marcus Buckingham and Curt Coffman state that "measurement always improves performance."

Franchisee Jim Lewis commented on the idea of measurement and its importance to the standards of the system: "The brilliance of McDonald's is detailing every standard and measuring it. Measurement is everything. If you are part of a system and it is not judged, well then, it's whoever can talk the best or manipulate the best that will win. In a system with standards and that has judgment on those standards, the truly best will rise to the top."

The system's emphasis on measurement became evident to me early on in my career. From the hourly readings to the daily sales, to how many bags of potatoes were used in a day, measurement was clearly an early lesson for all of us. It allowed an unbiased, objective look at how the operating system was doing. It sounds simple, but my experience has shown me that the process is far more uncommon than you might think. As a consultant today, I am constantly working with organizations to integrate metrics into their goals to allow for accurate review of their performance. So far, I have not found a task that I could not measure, and as former New York City mayor Rudy Giuliani famously said in a *New York Times* article, "If you can't measure something, then you cannot manage it." He should know. Under his watch as mayor of New York City, along with William Bratton, his police commissioner at the time, Giuliani took a simple process and revolutionized police performance. CompStat (COM-Paritive STATistics) is the accountability process that the department has been using since 1994. By measuring on a timely basis and by holding the precinct commanders accountable, and redeploying resources as needed, the amount of crimes in each precinct has dropped significantly. It serves as a model that any organization can adopt. Simply put, establish the goal, hold people accountable, work collaboratively to achieve goals, measure the results in a timely manner, and recognize the success. The peer pressure to perform is leveraged in this exercise to its fullest. McDonald's used this competitiveness and the spirit to challenge each other to a great degree of success.

At McDonald's, we learned about the importance of measurement early on in sales, in profits, in customer counts, in turnover percentage of crew, and a dozen other areas. This constant review of key metrics helped to develop many of our staff members into competent, effective managers. Ray Kroc was famous for asking what your volume was and how business was performing. He was genuinely interested, and that kept us on our toes. You never knew how he, or other executives after him, would question you. We always knew our numbers. And it made folks like me understand that the key to running a business is to understand how it's performing. And in the final analysis, that is done by clear, objective metrics.

Lesson Learned

Measurement. Always insist that goals have key metrics. Define them. Explain them. Measure them. Celebrate their achievement.

Measurement also served to disprove any falsehoods in the field in the occasional struggle to get operators to comply with standards. It was a tool Ed Rensi used when determining why owner/operators tried to avoid keeping up with new equipment requirements. "When we first got into the new shake machines the franchisees were concerned about it. They said it was hard to tear down, it's this and that." As Ed tells it, he set out to assess precisely why the franchisees were having so much difficulty with the shake machines: "I roamed around the stores, and the crew wasn't having any trouble with it. It seemed the franchisees didn't want to spend the money, and they were using the fact that it was difficult to set up and tear down as an excuse not to make the investment. So I started a contest at Hamburger University to put the machine together *blindfolded*! All of a sudden we had folks putting the damn machine together in seven minutes. I just found a way to take their argument, counter it, and defeat it."

Ed makes a valuable point, one that you will read about repeatedly throughout this book: Find out what is really happening in the field by visiting the locations and seeing what the real issues are—by the people who are closest to the action. You'll know quickly if your strategies are working, or if they need tweaking or, perhaps, rethinking.

Yet, measurement alone will not ensure success. And like most things, it can be taken too far. One of Fred Turner's legendary traits was his propensity to go against conventional wisdom. He admonished many of us if our real estate numbers (the estimated sales of a new store versus the actual sales after it opened) were *too good*. He felt that we were "not taking enough chances" and we shouldn't be so concerned with the statistics. Instead, he encouraged us to use "our gut and our instincts" more. He was concerned that we would be "playing by the numbers when, in the end, the most important element is the judgment of the person who says yes or no."

Standards That Won't Quit

We were always out to make the system better. It's an old habit that won't quit, even for ex-executives no longer with the company. As McDonald's former division president Debra Koenig put it: "You'd be walking into any McDonald's restaurant, anywhere, as a customer, but you would be picking up the butts in the parking lot, the trash on your way in. You're there as a customer, but you would be bussing the tables and you would perhaps say to your family members to wipe down those tables as well. I found myself doing that for multiple years."

Retired senior executive vice president and chief marketing officer Paul Schrage mused on the same topic: "I can't imagine anyone going into a restaurant and seeing a piece of paper and hesitating to pick it up . . . any officer. No questions, it was just something that was ingrained in you; the system is based on quality, service, cleanliness, and value. And that's part of it, and you just do it."

Ernie Annibale, a former director of development, reminded me that within our region we had developed a practice to constantly do a "postmortem" with the development staff, after a store opened, to see how the store was doing versus our projections. This exercise enabled us to learn from our past. The point was to discover how we could *move the bar higher* in our performance. I, too, was infused with the spirit of constant improvement. In the book *Good to Great*, Jim Collins writes about "continually refining the path to greatness with the brutal facts of reality." He may as well have been writing about McDonald's and our own internal forces to be tough on ourselves.

"Do It Right"

McDonald's focus on standards became obvious to me on day one, when I started as crew. I noticed that all the windows were cleaned daily, inside and out, and the concrete walkway was scrubbed and washed every day. All the bathrooms were cleaned till they were spotless. The stainless steel throughout the kitchen was polished every night. Garbage bins were not only emptied but scrubbed, inside and out, every day. There were strict guidelines for each position in the store, and the maintenance position was no exception. And it was a position of great importance within the store hierarchy. Rick McCoy, a retired operator, stated to me, "A good maintenance man can make an operation, and can make a manager. You buy with the eye, and people want to see a shiny store." The guidelines for the maintenance position were spelled out in the operations manual, as well as in early years, a training filmstrip, and were of course communicated through new technological mediums as they advanced. The thoroughness was evident, which even included the correct way to clean a toilet! (Did you know that the lip under the toilet bowl needs to get scrubbed daily to prevent buildup?) The idea of cleanliness was driven at all levels. One of the favorite sayings was: "If you have time to lean, you have time to clean."

Roland Jones, in his book *Standing Up & Standing Out*, reflecting on his career at McDonald's as both an employee and a franchisee, had his own thoughts on the importance of standards within the system: "My reason for concentrating on upgrading the physical environment was straightforward. I believe that physical appearance affects not only the impression outsiders have of a person or a business but also the way that the person or business functions. The environment influences how people think, and it is very difficult to maintain enthusiasm for a job when the work environment is drab, dirty, and disorganized." Roland makes a valid point. When an organization doesn't make the effort to physically look its very best, it loses out on more than customers; it also misses opportunities to connect with quality vendors and talent in its staff.

I realized quickly that McDonald's had a "system" for every aspect of the business, and it struck a chord with me in my young career development. My grandfather, who emigrated from Sicily to the United States as a young teenager, used to tell me, "If you are going to do something, do it right." Maybe this was the sentiment of his generation, but clearly Ray and Fred shared that same attitude, and they built the McDonald's system on it. Fred's legendary intensity on the details memorialized these standards for the system.

Ray articulated well when he commented, "In the early days when we couldn't get people to have confidence in buying a 15-cent hamburger, I said, 'I'm going to have that place so clean that they've got to have confidence in what we're producing,' and we've kept it that way and we're going to keep it that way." Both Ray and Fred's penchant for standards are evident throughout the company. Take, for example, Hamburger University. Founded in 1961, this state-of-the-art facility is the first of its kind in the fast-food industry. It includes teaching rooms, multiple auditoriums, and special equipment rooms as well as rooms to promote team integration. What's more, Hamburger University runs labs where managers learn to improve their game. McDonald's is considered the nation's largest training facility—surpassing even the U.S. Army! Training occurs at every restaurant in every region at all levels. And more than 100,000 McDonald's employees have traveled to Hamburger University in Oak Brook, Illinois, which trains 5,000-plus students each year; in addition, there are six other such facilities worldwide. And just a few miles away from the Oak Brook facility is McDonald's Innovation Center, where, among other practices, a store anywhere across the globe can send in its receipts for a given day so that experts can run through the orders during that time period and analyze how to quicken the pace so that customers are better served while the product maintains its quality. "Good enough" is never acceptable—a team, and an individual, can always do better. And McDonald's puts the resources to drive that performance increasingly up. As mentioned in the book *In Search of Excellence* by Tom Peters, Fred Turner created a "no-excuses environment."

Another example of continuous improvement over the years is the use of suppliers and vendors to collaborate with the company at improving its systems for delivery and product quality. As mentioned in John F. Love's book *Behind the Arches*, "In their search for improvements, McDonald's operations specialists moved back down the food and equipment supply chain. They changed the way farmers grow potatoes and the way companies process them. They introduced new methods to the nation's dairies. They altered the way ranchers raised beef and the way the meat industry makes the final product. They invented the most efficient cooking equipment the food service industry had ever seen."

A Culture Steeped in Excellence

I had no way of knowing this at the time, of course, but I was experiencing a very deliberate culture. There's a saying at McDonald's: "Ray dreamt it, and Fred built it." Take the french fries, a detail you can clearly taste, famously praised by the chef Julia Child. Though the standards have changed because of new dietary trends, it was Fred and his passion for standards that enabled the system to create McDonald's fries, celebrated around the world for its consistent excellence. Fred worked closely with growers and pushed for proper storage temperatures at a time when such standards weren't pursued by restaurant chains. In 1957, Louis Martino, an owner/operator in Glen Ellyn, Illinois—and the husband of June Martino, Ray's original secretary who was keenly instrumental at working with the early executive team and helping to guide the company's growth in those early years—created a food lab, perfecting the formula for consistent french fries. That level of research and development was unheard of for a fledgling fast-food company. But it was an early indicator of what would follow: the company's Innovation Center as well as a restaurant research kitchen facility where recipes and processes are challenged in the company's continued quest for excellence, and for more than 32 years McDonald's has had an executive chef on board working the recipes and exploring new products. All told, the company spent upward of $3 million developing its renowned french fries in the mid-1950s—again paving the way for a culture that demanded nothing but the best. As just one example, today, the beef supply is inspected from the farm to the restaurant, undergoing 2,000 quality and safety checks before arriving at a restaurant.

And while Fred is largely recognized as the guy behind the standards, he is the first to point out that he had help along the way. "You can't do a food standard without Nick Karos' name," he said of Nick, an aeronautical engineer by training, who was hired by Ray to develop field operations with Fred, and later became a franchisee. It was Nick's precision that enabled Fred to raise the bar, especially with respect to the standards of quality. "When it came to food and standards, it was he and I together. I get credit, but I didn't do it alone. He was in on it every step of the way." Raising the bar is one thing, but as Fred pointed out, you need fresh insights to make a difference.

Frank Kuchuris, a longtime supplier of buns to the McDonald's system, had this to say about standards: "Much of the progress of the bakery in my viewpoint has been because of McDonald's. They asked and always got the quality they expect versus the quality that was just accepted out there. Standards of the system today are so great and so much further ahead."

Fred's push for excellence is evident in McDonald's first operations manual, which he wrote in 1958. On page 11 of that original manual, he wrote: "Drive-in employees *can be* and *are being* trained to do a job and do it well. But they must be convinced that we believe the job they are doing is a respectable, first-rate occupation and one that offers a future as a McDonald's manager or owner." Even in those early years, the lure of opportunity was prevalent. This strategy also helped retain employees. Good people will stick around if they sense opportunity. And once again, that culture has stood the test of time. Sixty-seven thousand managers and assistant managers working today started as crew members. In an environment where the average employee changes jobs six times in his or her career, the amount of tenured staff at McDonald's is remarkable—especially today.

Fred never let up on standards. In the third edition of the operations manual, according to John F. Love's *Behind the*

Arches, Fred wrote: "YOU MUST BE A PERFECTIONIST! There are hundreds and hundreds of details to be watched. There isn't any compromising. Either (A) the details are watched and our volume grows, or (B) you are not particular, not fussy, and do not have pride or liking for the business. In which case you will be an also-ran. If you fall into the 'B' category, this is not the business for you."

Capturing the Meaning of Standards

While serving as a director of operations for my franchisee, the corporation decided to put together a film (in 16-millimeter format, no less) about the organizations—including ours—that consistently produced "A" stores, featuring interviews with those who followed best practices. The moderator asked one of my supervisors, who had been quiet most of the time, what he thought the key to our success was. The camera focused in on him, he reflected for a moment or so, and then blurted out: "We are never satisfied." Little did he realize the wisdom of his comment. To this day, I believe that phrase is a key to any organization's ultimate achievements, and helped to epitomize the culture of the relentless pursuit of excellence I was learning.

Strengthening the Brand

Standards made the brand enticing not only to consumers but also to prospective owner/operators who wanted to see return on investment. "What goes with the standard is trust," said Ron Bailey, a New York operator. "If you have a trusted brand, it doesn't matter where you are, you know that you're going to get the same product in the South Bronx that you're going to get on Long Island." As Ron pointed out, the owner/operators commit to following the standards by signing the licensing agreement, and recognize that if they don't, the entire system is compromised. If a consumer has a bad experience at a store in the Bronx, they will have the same poor impression about the store on Long Island, or anywhere else, for that matter. "That's why the link has to always be the same. Each link has to carry its own weight," Ron noted. "The liability extends to all franchisees. You can't have one or two who says, 'I'm not going to test my meat or follow a beef integrity process because there's a liability.' The standards have to apply to everyone and have to be followed by everyone."

There are, of course, financial pressures in following those standards, and some owners will grumble about the time and money needed to achieve those high standards. But on the whole, they understand the value behind their investment at operating superior restaurant operations. As Ron put it, "We looked at theorists who don't have standards and businesses that do whatever they want to do. And they fail. And they have this domino effect when that happens."

McDonald's standards are no surprise to prospective franchisees. "What's key in McDonald's for the franchisee is the interview process. The expectations, what this is about and what you are willing to do," Ron said. "So as long as you understand coming in all the things that you have to do—I may have to mop and that's why the on-the-job training program and also the training program that franchisees go through—you get to see it and feel it. Then you have a choice. The training is up to two years. That's a long enough time to decide: Do I really want to do this? If you spend two years and you still want to do it, then you should be in."

Still, operators and managers sometimes had trouble living up to those standards. If their business did not draw a crowd, as was the case in one of the first restaurants I managed (it was in an up-and-coming neighborhood, which initially was under-populated), it was hard to earn the revenue needed to keep the store humming. These restaurants were designed to do volume—

and if you didn't have the customer base or right location to ring up enough sales to perform above the breakeven point, it was tough to balance the bills and maintain standards. It was a challenge for sure, but the best operators used ingenuity to get past this hurdle, something I'll talk about in Chapter 4.

Breaking Records

"We take the hamburger business more seriously than anyone else," Ray Kroc said, and his words became my mantra from day one. I worked my way up to grill person, the key position, after many months and had a pretty good knack for speed and dexterity, always striving to perform up to the standards expected of me. Coworkers and I raced to see who was fastest at flipping the burgers and putting patties on the grill. I could usually hold my own. But the more important contests were sales. We strove to break any record . . . hourly, daily, or weekly. There was a bonus if you worked during that time period. And we broke records. Our store became one of the top sales restaurants in the area, and we got quite good at keeping the lines down and increasing sales. It was also important in the status of crew if you worked the "record" hour on your station. We fought to be there when the big crowds gathered for a chance to break the record on our shift. There was clearly some alpha male stuff going on within our group. I became a fixture on Saturdays, as that was our busiest day. One Saturday I took off work for a family event and my coworkers called me at home gloating that they had broken a new record hour and just "wanted to let me know." Of course, it had the intended effect of making me jealous of them, and I was riled up to "take it back" the following Saturday. It also made me decide to ditch the idea of going to my upcoming high school graduation ceremony and just work instead. Heck, the school could mail my diploma; the challenge of being there for another record breaking was far too tempting.

With the team so focused on "being the best," the competitive spirit was always present. Thanks to slogans and mottos within our store environment as well as our attitude that "only the best can work here," we developed the esprit de corps and pride attained by the best groups. These are traits any groups and organization can cultivate, regardless of its size or field of endeavor. Build that competitive spirit around a high set of performance standards and let the group dynamics lead you to higher levels.

Later in 1974, as a department head I became part of the "inner circle of leadership" within the regional organization. Although our meetings were infrequent, we were responsible for the budgets of our respective departments and accountable for results on the annual goals that we put together each year. My duties included forecasting, budgeting, people planning, goals and objectives, and salary administration. These were all areas I had touched on before, but not to this degree. As with most things McDonald's, there were strict policies and procedures and manuals for almost everything, and these items were no exception. There were ratios and standards to follow for most activities. Follow the book, ask for input, and add your own common sense, and you will make it. I plodded my way through.

The push for operational excellence permeated the entire organization. Years later, when I served as regional manager running a "State of the Region" annual event for owner/operators and key staff, I stressed operational excellence as a requirement that operators must demonstrate in order to open additional units. This point was nonnegotiable. We even instituted our own "top gun" for the owner/operators to reeducate themselves in the basics of store operations in a low-stress, fun, and involved competition along with our field staff.

Lesson Learned

Take a tour. As much as we preached to be "visible and on the floor" in the thick of the activities occurring in the store, we also stressed the importance of both walking around the perimeter of the restaurant and spending time in the dining room. Early on, Ray implored managers to be outside of the kitchens. Many of our managers resisted this role as they felt more comfortable "behind" the counter, not in front of it. It was a constant battle to teach them the importance of getting out and around, a strategy described by *In Search of Excellence* author Tom Peters as "management by walking around." Our version of this activity, while seemingly innocent enough, actually allowed great opportunity to observe how the restaurant was operated from both a customer's and a critical point of view.

We focused on a number of areas in our tours: staff and crew, the physical plant, customers, the movement of cars in the drive-thru and the customers at the counter, the detail cleanliness, the dining room temperature and lighting, the lot lights and signage, the restroom condition, the condition of the parking lot, and more. We constantly collected information, some to be used immediately, some for later that shift, and some for consideration at another time. It allowed for an opportunity to recognize both individual and team effort, always with an eye on the activities of the staff. And our goal was to do this every 30 minutes! Vigilance was constant.

No matter whether you are responsible for one location or hundreds of them, a skilled assembly line or an office full of employees, or a crew on a construction site, getting out and around and being visible is an important part of leadership. It shows that you genuinely care.

By growing up in a standards-enriched system, we were able to rise to each new challenge again and again. Take the late Jim Cantalupo, a 28-year McDonald's veteran who came out of retirement to return to the company as CEO, and who Fred Turner today still describes as "so outstanding." Jim's background in architecture gave him "a sense of what is a good-looking store, and what does it take to have a good-looking store," Fred notes. "Jim had a background in accounting, coming in from the financial end, but he gained his McDonald's experience in the line positions." He had enough of an aptitude for it and also an interest in it. He had a tremendous aptitude for marketing and also operations as well. By the time he was in the chair as the . . . CEO of international, he had an operational background and an operational backbone and an operational marketing acumen," Fred notes. Having a field operations background "is a real strength at McDonald's. The top management team [must have] that base of experience; it makes a huge difference when you don't have it and you see a lot of problems developing. I could see that in McDonald's China, when it didn't have a sufficient number of strong operations-based and operation-experience-based people in the senior management. . . . That previous team . . . could speak Mandarin, [which] was great with the government, great with the press, great in getting companies interested in McDonald's; [they] did some great stuff but just didn't relate to operations at all." Things turned around, Fred says, when the company brought in an operations person skilled in training and with an aptitude for McDonald's standards.

Standards were always dictated by delivering the best possible customer experience. And no matter how widely these standards set forth by McDonald's were spelled out, there were times that a franchisee or a manager running a company store did not live up to them, despite the level of one-on-one coaching and mentoring. It was always interesting to me to see just how high a particular franchisee's standard of cleanliness really was. Coming from a strict Italian family where personal hygiene, particularly around food, was very important, this proved to be an interesting learning experience. Putting a quarter under a grill, just to see if it was discovered, as the grill was on schedule to be removed for cleaning on a weekly basis, was only one of the tricks we employed to keep an eye on how diligently operators lived up to our standards. The vast majority of licensees accepted the high standards, and to their credit, they did a great job and taught us in the process how well they could run operations. Others never seemed to understand our passion. Never mind that these franchisees would never open another unit—by not honoring the standards, they risked their right to stay in the system. Those few were pushed out of the system and let go, and the stories leaked out that let every owner know that McDonald's was very serious about QSC.

81

Case in Point

How important are maintaining standards to an organization? The standards set are vital to the trust you develop with your consumer. There are a lot of ramifications to not upholding tight standards. Consider the case of Raymond Dayan, a McDonald's operator who had the exclusive territory in Paris, France. As noted in John F. Love's *Behind the Arches*, Dayan had defied McDonald's QSC standards.

Field inspectors graded the stores with an F rating, having found dirty sites where menu items were not prepared with the prescribed recipes and the food—cooked in stale oil—was served up cold and unappealingly. McDonald's sought to buy out Dayan's restaurants and franchise territory, and when

Dayan refused, the corporation disfranchised him. In response, Dayan filed a lawsuit, but the court ruled in McDonald's favor. As Love wrote: "When [McDonald's] needed to adapt Ray Kroc's principles of fairness to a larger and more complex system, it was willing and able to bend. When it had to protect those principles from attack by those who ignored them, it was ready to wage war."

McDonald's would wage war publicly so that its significance was evident to all. "There were consequences to not adhering to the standard," notes Burt Cohen, a retired senior vice president of licensing. And as Debra Koenig put it, "People needed to know that there were consequences to those consumer experiences, and every once in a while we would have to say goodbye to a franchisee." This of course was never easy. As Debra reminded me, "You would wonder as a member of the corporation, did I warn them enough, did I coach them enough? Did I give them enough opportunities to hear?" Yet these kinds of decisions were essential to protecting the brand. "It was never personal," Debra pointed out. "It was never about that executive in charge of those company stores or that particular franchisee. It was all about the consumer experience, or lack thereof—and then moving forward to find the resolutions, whether that was improving the situation or saying good-bye."

As much as our instincts were to praise the good, we clearly focused on what wasn't right. "No McDonald's person that walks into a restaurant doesn't walk in to critique," noted Kathy May, who runs training at Hamburger University in Oak Brook. "We find what's not right, even though there may be 100,000 things that are right." I can remember spending time in the field showing operators and their staff what we called "dumpster diving" (a practice that was early on demonstrated by Ray Kroc himself), which meant looking in the wastebaskets and finding out what people were throwing out. While the practice was unsavory at best, it revealed the need to be always vigilant to what the customer was telling us silently about our food, and that led to many a review of basic operations in those restaurants where issues were discovered.

This proactive stance was embraced at the top. As Ed Rensi explains: "I want to know the problems today. I don't want pimples to turn into boils. Tell me the bad news yesterday. Good news I could wait six months for. Because good news isn't a threat. Bad news is a problem. I always said this my whole life: 'Do the hard things first, because the easy stuff gets really easy.' Nobody wants to do the hard stuff first." We embraced tackling "the hard stuff" first. No heads in the sand. No wishing problems would resolve themselves. It's that very standard that helped build McDonald's, leaving competitors behind.

One on One with Fred Turner

To this day, standards of the system are on Fred Turner's mind, all the time. Even as the honorary chairman, it is held clearly as a passion. And there is nothing more critical than McDonald's fries to our customers. As Fred and I sat and discussed fries, his concern over the latest dietary trends, and some subtle taste differences, I sensed a deep concern. His voice changed and his head dropped, and he actually got emotional, shedding a tear with me on this conversation.

Taken aback, I realized the depth of this man's passion for high standards. No wonder generations of McDonald's leadership has been "obsessed" with quality. McDonald's has a legacy of passion as exemplified by Fred Turner to this day.

A Stumble

In the early years of the 2000s, McDonald's was considered to have lost its way somewhat. From decreasing sales to diminishing consumer interest and increased competition, the company had lost its luster. As the *New York Times* reported, by January 2003 McDonald's reported its first quarterly loss. That same month, when Jim Cantalupo was called back from retirement and voted in as chairman and CEO, he immediately got to work to get the company on track. He understood the need to get back to basics and get the system back to its roots of QSC. In a *Nation's Restaurant News* article of February 18, 2003, he stated rather bluntly: "Clean restrooms and hot fresh food served in our restaurants would be a change." The company renewed its focus on the customer, and that shift helped the company boost earnings to $2.28 billion in 2004, up from $1.47 billion in 2003, according to *Nation's Restaurant News*. This growth stemmed from the company's "Plan to Win" strategy, which boils down to five P's: People, Products, Place, Price, and Promotion. These attributes incorporated the company's longstanding commitment to QSC. As Harvard Business School points out in a case study published in 2007, the new plan was "framed around the customer's every need and desire." Though I was no longer with McDonald's by this time, the news reaffirmed everything I'd been taught by the system about the importance of standards.

Spillover into Our Personal Lives

We lived and breathed so many standards that for many of us there was a spillover into our personal lives. We organized our homes and our private offices with precision. To this day, for example, I always ensure that there is backup supply for personal care items like toothpaste simply because I grew up in a system where running out of stock was verboten. And it wasn't just me who found McDonald's high regard for standard influencing the hours they spent outside of the job. "The principles that you use in McDonald's guide your life. You use them throughout your life. You become a better person," Frank Behan notes. "Lack of discipline will kill you," he adds. "You can't live a life without discipline." That discipline folded into your identity as a leader, and back at work we strived for culture where only excellence would suffice.

The best of us took "never be satisfied" personally, a practice that drove Jim Skinner to the top office of McDonald's. Jim has made a practice of writing his personal goals, along with his corporate goals, every year as a means of raising *his* expectations. Jim used to share his goals with Jim Cantalupo, who was at that point CEO. Jim Cantalupo questioned Jim Skinner as to why he was sharing his goals, to which Jim Skinner would reply, "I want you to know what I want to get better at, and I'm working on this to get better.'" Jim Skinner, in fact, is meticulous about putting things to paper, a practice that can be attributed to the standards and responsibility he takes as a leader. He spoke with me about this: "I'm in a meeting and I'm taking notes, every meeting, out of respect for people. Jim would say, 'Why are you writing that down?' I'd say, 'Because I want to understand what you and I talked about when I leave the room.'"

But Jim, Frank, and others I spoke to in writing this book aren't the only ones to recognize just how far that discipline can get you—especially at McDonald's. As Bill Cosby said in his commencement address to Cheyney University's Class of 2007, workers at McDonald's pick up many skills. "If I'm flipping burgers," Cosby noted, "I'm not flipping burgers for the rest of my life. I'm learning to become the manager. And I'm not the manager forever because I'm learning to become the regional manager." Cosby accurately depicted opportunities at McDonald's—for those, it should be stressed, who adhere to McDonald's rigorous standards.

That adherence to standards is something I've brought into my professional life, post-McDonald's. In my consulting practice today, we are always looking at how a task is measured and where the bar is set. It's important to clearly delineate what is acceptable, be that behavior, product quality, customer relations, marketing—that's part of the culture of any organization. It articulates what level of product you will accept. And I'm hardly alone in this practice. For instance, Debra Koenig, former divisional president, in her stint as CEO of Vicorp, said McDonald's commitment to QSC and also V (value), were attributes worth bringing to her next professional position. "I tried to take what McDonald's provided—great training at the service level and crew level, food that had to be served hot and tasty—and tried to apply those concepts to Vicorp," she says. "We applied a lot of those learnings from McDonald's around food and value to the menu."

A Final Thought

The passion for high standards is still prevalent within the system today—more than 50 years after Ray Kroc opened his first unit in Des Plaines. I've been asked many times in conversations, "How is it continued, how does the legacy stay strong?" While there is no simple answer, it seems that a number of actions continue to foster the legacy. One is the stories retold to numerous staff over and over again, exaggerated or not, giving credence to the notion that McDonald's values high standards. Another is the current executive team, including CEO Jim Skinner, which comes from a deep operations background and continues to set the pace and example for the entire organization. Also, the addition of "mystery shops," which are unannounced visits that are randomly executed to objectively determine a store's operational levels; sometimes these are conducted by an outside firm, establishing an even deeper understanding of how stores are performing as well as offering a more objective view in many cases. And the operator base, as well as the chain of vendors, is all mindful of how "we got here" and the importance of vigilance and continuous monitoring to ensure the high standards are met.

In Summary

Perhaps it is McDonald's passion for excellence and its quest to never be satisfied that put the company at the top of the industry. Without having high standards—and measurement—McDonald's never would have struck upon its formula for fries and burgers. It never would have achieved consistency from store to store. And it never would have achieved its level of QSC. Along with the standards grew a culture to be the best—whether it was in operations or slashing energy costs—so long as the end result did not detract from the customer experience. Organizations that push for continued excellence in all likelihood will improve profit margins while also boosting their reputations where it counts—among loyal customers, the best talent, and dedicated vendors.

87

Key Learnings

✔ Never accept any standard but the very best. "Good enough" won't cut it in today's competitive world. Continually challenge the team to improve the product. Keep your expectations high.

✔ Focus on, and develop your organization's strengths—don't allow your competitors to dominate your focus.

✔ If you see something wrong, fix it. Your actions set the standards. Problems don't resolve themselves.

✔ Create a career track for employees so that ultimately your organization will be led by those who have only the highest standards, coupled with the execution and achievement of those goals.

✔ Develop standards that ultimately result in delivering the best environment for both staff and customers.

4

Lead by Example

Leadership means developing and demonstrat-
ing to the people underneath you that you are
first of all entirely sincere, and that you are hon-
est and that you will subject yourself to any-
thing that you ask them to do, or you have
already proven yourself . . .

—Ray Kroc

Ray Kroc was an established legend in the food service arena by 1978, the year I first met him.

It was a night I will never forget.

On this particular occasion, I learned Ray was coming to New York, and as was his practice, he liked to visit with the regional folks whenever possible. Because the zone manager was busy, and at the time there was no regional manager, it was decided that I, as the director of operations, would be having dinner with Ray. Ray's secretary called me personally and let me know the details. He would be staying at the UN Plaza hotel in midtown, and would have Al Golin, his longtime public relations resource, with him. We would dine at the renowned 21 Club, a former speakeasy in Manhattan. In anticipation I immediately started thinking about which suit I would wear and how to handle myself.

Arriving at the hotel at the appointed time, I was all spit and polish, anxious as to how the evening would go. I watched as a large stretch limo pulled up and out bounded Ray himself, finely groomed with an air of confidence about him, walking right up to me and saying, "Hi Paul, I look forward to dinner with you tonight. I just want to go up and freshen up and I will be down in a minute." Naturally, I said, "Of course, Mr. Kroc," figuring it was best to show respect even though everyone at the company was on a first-name basis. Immediately, he insisted I call him "Ray."

When he returned, we got into the limo. I went for one of the "flip seats"—two small seats hinged to the front bench seat, which allowed additional passengers to sit, facing the rear seats. As I went to sit in one, Ray objected, saying, "You are my guest tonight. I'll sit there. You sit in the comfortable seat." That pretty much blew me away, and I sank into the deep lushness of the rear seat of the limo—my first ride ever in a limousine—while he took the uncomfortable hard seat. This offered a glimpse about humility and graciousness, no matter if you are one of the richest men in America, and the head and founder of the most successful restaurant organization in the world. It was a mindset I hoped I could incorporate as my own, in my professional life.

At the 21 Club, a spot I had only read about in the society pages, Ray was greeted warmly by the maître d, and suddenly I felt part of a circle of power I'd never before imagined. As he walked through the bar, stopping to show me how the hats and toys adorned the ceiling, I sensed the gaze of diners everywhere. Maybe it was his San Diego Padres ring, signifying the team he owned and loved. Or perhaps it was the aura and energy that just flowed from him. Regardless, the diners seemed to know they were in the presence of a true celebrity. After dinner, Ray insisted I have a tour of the basement, which featured a secret door where liquor was kept during prohibition and a wine cellar, where bottles were stored for Richard Nixon at the time. And while I relished the evening, what I treasured even more was

Ray's graciousness and the extent he went to to make me feel special. Here he was, a man who I heard so much about, but that night he made one of his thousands of employees feel valued. I walked away with a fresh perspective on the culture of the company I was now a part of, and with an understanding of how simply extending courtesies to someone can be so inspiring. In conversation, it was clear to me that Ray was not just motivated by money. He was motivated by a passion for his business and seeing it grow. He understood the value of having a great team and getting them to understand his vision and his principles. This was definitely something to emulate.

Did Ray have an idea of his profound impact on me, such a young executive at the time? I would argue yes. His conduct and his business principles spoke volumes. Leading by example—that was a trait that grew organically within the organization, ultimately becoming one of the clear "roots" of the company. I believe the practice came naturally to him, and that it grew within the organization.

But he developed a lead-by-example culture that continues to touch everyone. Peter Grimm, a longtime supplier with McDonald's, described something he saw in 2006, at the last operator convention in Orlando. It was the end of an evening at Universal Studios and everyone was leaving. "There I see Fred on his golf cart picking up trash. There were cups, and he was going around picking them up and putting them in the garbage. I saw it with my own eyes." That's what the McDonald's culture is all about.

Setting the Tone

Ray led by example from the very beginning. When he ran his own store in Des Plaines, Illinois, he moonlighted on weekends as the maintenance man, scrubbing the restaurant clean, and picking up the grounds. It's an era Fred Turner hasn't forgotten.

"I was training with operators, you know, working the store," Fred told me. "On Saturday morning Ray Kroc came in with a toothbrush. He got up on the sink, and he was scrubbing the holes in the mop wringer with this toothbrush. I saw him do that. It's true, he'd go around with his knife and scrape the gum off the cement. He certainly set the tone on appearance and provided a smarter way of doing things. So he looked at McDonald's more or less from the customers' point of view. Or the public's point of view. That's how the public viewed us and how they looked in on us."

And there are other stories as the former chief marketing officer Paul Schrage revealed. One involved Ray getting off the train, walking to the store, and picking up trash off the street along the way. "That had to resonate amongst all the people in the company," Paul said. And Bob Vidor, a former store manager at the time, shared a tale in which Ray, touring the New Jersey region, stopped at the store. "Let's go look at your lot," Ray said, and walked with some of the team members showing them what to look for, including cigarette butts. "The lesson was this was also our 'dining room,'" Bob told me. "Ray wasn't afraid to pick it up, so why should we be? It took about 15 minutes, and he said that the store looked good. He got in the limo and left." Ray fastidiously set the tone for cleanliness. These images are hard to dismiss, even today.

Lesson Learned

The most effective way to pass down a legacy is to work side by side with the future generation of leaders. Studies show that people absorb twice as much through hands-on learning as opposed to simply attending lectures or reading. Teach through your actions—it's the surest way to transfer knowledge.

Ray's lead was easy to follow, and that made it easy for others to subscribe to the direction he set for the system. It wasn't hard to know what to do—though you felt the pressure to have your game on. As Irv Klein, a retired longtime franchisee, explained to me: "When Fred did walk in your store, or Ray came in, it scared you to death, but at the same time, it made you feel you were really part of something." The company's commitment to QSC was demonstrated throughout the system—and we strived to honor the same mission that the top executives believed in.

Ray, the owner of the San Diego Padres, adopted the same approach with that team, Ed Rensi reminded me. "One game was just hideous, and Ray went into the pressroom and got on the PA system and said, 'I apologize to the 40,000 people in the stands about what crummy baseball the Padres were playing.' He wanted us to stop off at the ticket booth, so he could refund all our money because we shouldn't have to pay for such garbage. Talk about leading by example, honesty, and integrity. You look at these little stories and they imply what these guys believed. You've got to act like who you want to be."

93

Ed and others who worked closely with Ray always knew where he stood. "He had the native ability to lead," Ed said, "much more so than I think he ever realized. But he was a man who was very influential [with] other men. Part of that was being a sales manager. Leading by example—well, that's Ray."

Don Horowitz, retired executive vice president of the legal department, made this interesting observation to me: "They taught management in the restaurants, and they were really watching the operation and talking to the crew and knew what the hell was going on at the lowest level. I think that was a huge difference."

Ron Bailey, a six-store operator, said to me, "We still believe in the hands-on approach, from the regional manager to the business consultant. I always said *the speed of the leader determines the rate of the pack*. So when your crew sees you picking up a mop and mopping and not saying 'will you do this for me?' and actually doing it yourself . . . it sends out a message that if it's good for the goose, it's good for the gander. We started at the bottom, and look where we are, but we didn't forget where we came from."

That leadership was there for all to see, even if you didn't work in McDonald's, or, for that matter, were a Padres fan. During a Phil Donahue interview, Phil asked Ray about his hands-on experience in growing the system. "Did you clean the toilets?" Phil asked. To which Ray replied, "You're damn right, I cleaned the toilets." Ray then added, "And I still would today if I saw a dirty one . . . in a McDonald's." Ray's message was loud and clear. All units must have clean bathrooms, and Ray wasn't above pitching in, if it meant getting the job done.

Ray walked the talk. He set the tone for both his standard of operations and his own willingness to do whatever it took to make McDonald's successful.

It's a philosophy Jim Cantalupo demonstrated as well during his tragically short tenure as CEO. Former McDonald's executive Claire Babrowski told me about a late Friday night strategy session in which they were updating the system's emergency action plan, in the event that the U.S. beef supply was ever put in question. Jim, who had gone home for a bit, returned because he knew the team was working late. After listening to the debate, he thanked the team for the hours they put in, and told them he knew they'd reach the right decisions. He said three things mattered: "how would it affect the operators, the restaurants, and the system." As he walked out, he turned around and said "and I didn't say profitability." It was a profound comment. Not many CEOs of a public company would put the operating system over profits—unless they understood, as Jim did, that it was the system that drove profits. And he wanted to make that point clear to his employees.

Clear Expectations, Demonstrated Everywhere

I picked up many ideas and thoughts on leading staff from observing the practices of leaders around me, and I applied those lessons when I managed the restaurant floor in the early years. The system seemed designed with specific expectations coupled with common sense. And I learned them soon enough. If employees didn't put their all into a task, whether it was working the grill or mopping the floor, I'd send them home—even if we were short-staffed. I'd sooner mop the floor myself than have workers undermine the efforts of our team. And as tough as that was to do, it sent a message that was so important . . . that if you were going to be part of the team, you had to be engaged and perform your assigned task up to our standards, as I was demonstrating.

On the restaurant floor, there never was any question as to what was expected of us. Our managers for the most part enjoyed working with us in the store. They actually would work *alongside* of us. They would be shoulder to shoulder when it got busy. And at times that meant actually doing crew tasks; it also meant directing, pushing, complimenting, and communicating the entire time with the crew. I'm not sure those managers understood how powerful their actions really were. But it helped us to thrive. People want to be on a winning team. They seek to do right, to have someone recognize their skills and accomplishments. And there was an added benefit. Because the average age of a McDonald's manager was so young at the time (I was only 21 when promoted to manager), we were impressionable, perhaps to a much greater degree than managers in other organizations. That led to a deeper appreciation between mentor and crew and a further absorption of knowledge.

In his book *Standing Up & Standing Out*, Roland Jones, a founder of the National Black McDonald's Operators Association, as well as a former McDonald's franchisee and company employee, expressed these thoughts on mentoring: "Working alongside a store's employees, I was teaching them by example, demonstrating the company's standards and the benefits of doing things in a set way, and modeling problem solving. By working with store crews, I was showing them that *my* standards were McDonald's standards. I was raising the bar, and good workers rose to the challenge, meeting higher standards and claiming ownership in them."

Lesson Learned

Because all eyes are on you as a leader, you set the example and will be watched by all levels within your organization. So bearing in mind how impactful your activities can be to your audience, look for ways to continuously teach. It's a great time to coach and model the behaviors you value and want to see replicated.

As Tony Liedtke, a New York operator with seven stores, explained it: "I preach that service is omnipotent. [If] I walk in and I see someone not being served, I'll serve them. I don't say, 'Hey, we need someone over here.' I'll say that after I take the guy's order. So, when I tell them that I can't stand service issues, they've all seen me handle them." And by observing Tony, they learn how to navigate situations as they arise.

Constant Mentoring

For the most part, role models were everywhere. Many of our managers and supervisors served as models of excellence, and all we had to do was follow their lead. I found this to be true, too, as I worked my way up the ladder into corporate, where top leadership made it very clear what it took to get results.

I also learned from those who were not good managers, and absorbed what skills they lacked, and cataloged them so that I learned what not to do when I became manager.

And I wasn't the only one with this approach. Take, for example, former CEO Mike Quinlan, who shared this with me: "I was going up the ladder early. I looked around and I was always the youngest of everything," he said. "I looked around at all the people I did business with—operators, suppliers, company people— and observed that many were trying to get by, that some were in over their head, that some were too political, that some were kind of cheats; cheats could be a lot of things, a guy that would cheat on his expense account. When I was being trained as a field consultant, one of the guys who trained me would say, 'Okay, you can go to dinner and have a couple of extra drinks and you could put it on your expense account, you could do this and do that,' and I thought, no way. And the operators—I used to watch the guys I dealt with even before I was a field consultant, I watched some of them maneuvering and trying to cheat their way, and you look and you learn. So, I looked and I learned a lot by *watching people*—good, bad, and indifferent—and how they do it. And the ones who had the courage to do the right thing and the ability to know what the right thing was, and the courage to do it, were the ones I followed and respected. And one by one, the others, you know, they fall by the wayside."

Mentoring was shown in other ways, by sharing the workload by the entire team. David Delgado, now a circuit court judge, recalled his years in the real estate legal department in Oak Brook. "I learned so much from my real estate manager, Bob. He had so much valuable information and was always willing to sit down and go over it step by step. I was not only told how to do something, I was shown how to do it. It was not about him as a manager sitting in the corner office, saying figure it out. I found that to be encouraging. And if I got inundated

97

with work, my supervisor would take some of the files, as would the vice president, to help, too."

Donn Wilson, who joined the company in 1957 by opening and owning the eighteenth McDonald's, went on to hold various field positions within the company, becoming managing director of McDonald's in Australia, and later moved on to much corporate success, including owning the Houston Astros. Donn had this to say about leading by example: "It was throughout the organization. Everybody got that from Ray because he set that example, absolutely. Fred, of course, carried it out to a great degree by getting into the restaurants and working shoulder to shoulder with you. When I went to Australia (to open up that market in 1970), that's again leading by example. I shared a hotel room and I made all of my people with different backgrounds, physical locations, and such do the same, and we developed that same camaraderie. Here I was, at the time one of the key executives of the company (Ray being the other) and I'm in there sleeping three to a room. You were forced to develop personal relationships." Donn lived and breathed the company's beliefs in cutting costs where possible, in building a team, and in diversity—qualities his team members were sure to notice.

Willis Smart, former regional vice president and now operations vice president for Dunkin Brands, expressed these thoughts: "Do what you say. I mean the importance of how you act to develop and change a culture. If you are trying to get people to think more often about sales, or operations, you have to walk the talk, you have to set an example, and when you are trying to get into a culture that doesn't do that, you cannot ever compromise it."

And former UK marketing chief officer Laurie Morgan shared this memory: Company executives when visiting stores were often "the first to grab the fry basket if fries are up and hands are full. Better yet, they'll grab the mop, clean up a spill, and schmooze all the customers while they are at it."

All along I found that nothing is more inspiring than when owners and key executives push up their sleeves to accomplish whatever is needed to get done. Irv Klein commented on a remark he had heard Fred Turner make on several occasions: "You don't understand the McDonald's business unless you work the McDonald's business." We followed that lead and made sure to be in the restaurants doing our best to serve customers.

Owner/operators were mentored too. Rick McCoy, at one time one of the largest franchisees in the system with 90 restaurants, recalled working with a mentor, a field representative, who "would just throw everything out if it didn't look good. I remember really dumping things, and after he did it about five or six times I would think, wow this guy is for real. It's not a show."

Prospective owner/operators spend up to two years training in stores for as much as 20 hours a week before learning if they will even be considered for a store. Not only did they learn what it meant to run a $2 million business, they also learned about McDonald's culture, where sharing knowledge is an expectation.

Behind the counter, I grew accustomed to working alongside my managers as well. As crew in my early years working for a franchisee, I remember the senior franchisee—to my teenage eyes, a much older gentleman—who had come into town to visit the stores would quickly get behind the counter and help to wrap burgers when we got busy, lending a hand and fostering a sense in us that *our* work was important. This was hardly an anomaly. Operators and managers worked together with crew during a rush, and for good reason. As Ed Rensi pointed out: "You could never get more out of people than you were willing to give of yourself to them. And if you aren't willing to get down there and respect dirty hands and sweat, then how can you expect those people with dirty hands and sweat to respect you?"

But you didn't just pitch in when needed. You took ownership of your job. That was the behavior you saw all around you.

And the by-product was well-trained people who did so much more than merely understand your role because of a published regulation, said longtime supplier Ted Perlman. "You find out more and more that *interaction shown by example* makes people responsible," he said.

Most operators grasped that they had a vested interest in leading by example. "The owners are there every day. Seven days a week, they're on site," Frank Behan pointed out. "Greeting customers, showing help what they stand for. That's what we had when we had Ray." And that was a legacy that was handed down from each successive management team.

Jim Skinner, current CEO, certainly got that message. He mentioned to me that "leadership by example at McDonald's may be one of the most important things we do. You have to walk the talk; you have to demonstrate through your leadership. They [the employees] want leaders, and they want people that are going to get up in the morning and behave in a way that their best interest is looked out for. I try to embrace that value and lead by example in everything I do."

That constant in-the-trenches experience combined with continuous mentoring and recognition helped propel McDonald's ahead of the competition. Stakeholders were too involved to ever risk being out of touch. Former divisional president Debra Koenig put it this way: "You absolutely have to be engaged in every experience, and so you can't be disengaged if you are in a McDonald's. Picking up the lot, bussing every table—I think that's true throughout, and I can't begin to tell you through all of my positions with McDonald's where you would jump behind the counter when they needed you."

Management at other companies are probably too ensconced in the executive suite to scrub a toilet as Ray had. They are not down in the trenches, seeing things as the public does. If the customer is truly the reason we're in business, all levels of management must interface with that customer by getting as close as possible to him or her. As Ed noted, at other organizations, "management is so removed from its workforce." My own consulting has shown that to be true. At one organization, a national chain of restaurants, the executive level was never involved in touring and visiting the restaurants and missed out on the benefits associated with these visits. While we tried to get them to understand the importance of this, and the benefits at all levels, ultimately they never got it. The business was soon sold after our discussions with them. There is no substitute for the truths you gather by observing in the field, and the importance of executives from the top leading by example. Take it from Andrew Carnegie, who once said, "As I grow older, I pay less attention to what men say. I just watch what they do."

Lessons Learned

There can be no greater motivator for an organization's leadership than to spend quality time closest to the customers and staff members who interact with them every day. The rewards are threefold. Executives benefit because they learn on the frontline. Staff members benefit by learning to exemplify behaviors. And the customers benefit because their overall experience usually improves by the leaderships' presence.

Frank Kuchuris, a longtime bun supplier for McDonald's and second generation in the business, summed it up well to me: "I have a routine. I never go into the office when I visit one of our plants. Every time I go, even though it is against the rules, I always go in the back door, and walk the plant from the back forward and say hello and chit chat because one of the biggest things is that they want to bring you in their office and give you coffee and the whole thing. But I remember this from Dad [who was exemplifying walking through the plant] and the system, you work and you're down there, you're one of them. Not the first time, it takes time, but all of a sudden they say, 'Hey.' They will say hello to you." As Frank understands, you're not just putting in face time; you're contributing to the cause and also bonding with the folks who are integral to the success of your business.

When visiting restaurants, I always maintained that even if the manager wore the same uniform as the crew, it should be obvious who was in charge by his or her actions on the floor. Working the restaurant floor is not a spectator sport—it's interactive. That readiness to pitch in at a moment's notice also mirrored the adage that all new management candidates follow—to lead by example. There is nothing more motivating to the staff than to see their leaders with them in the thick of the battle. True leaders are visible, active, and with their staffs—up front and personal. Those who study military history will remember that General Patton endeared himself to his troops by leading his tank brigade *on foot*. How inspiring was that!

In that same regard, Ed Rensi, as president of McDonald's, took leadership to heart. For many years, his business card read:

Chief Burger Griller, French Fryer, Shake Maker, Cheer Leader.

Ed's was a clear message: he was not above any of those tasks, as they were the key ingredients to serving our customers.

Never Looking the Other Way

Like so many other executives, Ed never hesitated to help out when in a restaurant that was busy. You could not, in good faith, look the other way from a serious service issue. That point was drilled into you. And the more adept you were as crew, the more credibility you earned, even if you worked in corporate but were visiting a restaurant as part of your field work. In my conversation with former CEO Jack Greenberg, he recounted a time he visited a store during a rush with the present CEO Jim Skinner. Jim had grown up in the system and was well versed in every operational nuance. But he had forgotten that Jack, who had entered the system in finance, had revved up to speed with the system by completing six months of intensive in-store operational training. Jack was on his game. Compelled to help out in a pinch, as is typical McDonald's style, Jim no doubt showing some compassion, suggested that Jack take fries; this was a relatively easy station to handle and, if Jack worked it, it was obvious that he would likely be able to really make a difference. Yet Jack, knowing his prowess was probably more current than Jim's said, "No, you take fries, I'll work in the back with the grill team." Jack's response sent Jim a subtle—and probably slightly surprising— message that he "could handle it" and was now operationally qualified. Here Jack was higher up the corporate ladder than Jim, yet he still wanted to show he could work the grill—and work it well. That ability was as important to crew as it was to corporate officers. They too prided themselves and were even competitive on their competent restaurant skills. In recounting this story to current CEO Jim Skinner, he laughed as he recalled, how after the visit, they jokingly sent the operator a bill for their "services" at their executive pay rate broken down in hours. That subtle, humorous, and creative approach helped to send the right messages about pitching in whenever needed in the right way.

And never mind the interaction between Jack and Jim. Imagine the message their presence sent to the crew. It let them know that management is accessible. Their style may be different but not necessarily better. It lets the crew know that everyone is in this as a family, and that together we can make a difference.

No Hierarchy

This basic tenet of leadership was hard for any manager worth their stuff to ignore. It was a classic understanding that you had to be on the floor. And this meant working with the crew, the customers, and, when needed, the stations. All McDonald's staff had this burned into their heads. The more you understood that, the greater your respect within the organization. As Vivian Ross, vice president of labor relations, said to me, "The field is the system." And she made sure that her team of lawyers could adapt to the store environment and that the crews in the field were comfortable with her team.

"I have always been schooled at McDonald's that it's about the restaurants, and I have always valued in my lawyers, the ones that have worked with me, in their ability to be able to be as comfortable in the crew room as they are in the board room," Vivian told me. " So, my guys have for the most part, been able to sit in the basement of a McDonald's restaurant crew room and be able to engage in a conversation with a crew person and make them feel comfortable and then be able to come back and report back to top management. To conduct yourself in a way that crew people would find offensive is counter to our culture."

Showing, Not Telling

Sometimes lessons are best taught with the fewest words possible, as Ed Rensi shared with me. He recalled in the early 1970s, working in Columbus, Ohio, "We were constantly being clobbered by companies starting new restaurants in Columbus. I mean, you name it, they started it there," Ed said, referring to up-and-comers including Arby's and Arthur Treacher's Fish and Chips. "At the time we didn't serve fish, and the Catholics were eating fish on Fridays. They were kicking our ass because they had really great fish. In Ohio people eat a lot of fish, plus Procter & Gamble were pushing their fish sticks. So we finally talk Ray and Fred into coming to Columbus to see Arthur Treacher's Fish and Chips." Ed and his associate, Tom, picked them up at the airport, and with Fred and Ray in the back seat, Ed stopped off at the Arthur Treacher's, ready to go in. But that was not to be, as Ed described: "Ray says, 'I'm not going in there.' With that, Ed turns to Fred, and Fred says, 'I'm not going in there. I never go into a competitor's restaurant. I am not spending my money in a competitor's restaurant.' I said, 'Well, what do you want to do?' He said, 'Well, you invited us down here.'" So Ed went into the store and bought some fish, and brought it back to the car for everyone to eat. He continued, "Ray says, 'I'm not eating that stuff.' Fred says, 'I'm not eating that stuff.' So Tom and I start eating and talking about it. Then Fred says, 'Take us back to the airport.'" So they did, and Ray and Fred flew back to Chicago.

The visit didn't last an hour and half, but Ed said he learned something valuable that day. "Ray wanted nothing to do with the stuff. Fred was making a point: stop worrying about the other guys and worry about yourself. He could have said, 'I'm not coming down there, I'm not going through these shenanigans.' But he knew the only way he was going to get that region to get off their high horse about our competitors was to come down there and do what he did."

As Ed saw, sometimes the best way to prove your point is to demonstrate it, up close and in person. You'll quickly see who gets your message, and you'll also demonstrate that you cared enough to mentor your people as to where to concentrate their efforts. That's not to say that the company didn't check on its competition. Of course, it did, as any business should. But Ray and Fred believed Ed was too concerned about the competition and not concentrating enough on what was transpiring in his own market.

Fred commented to me about this incident and said not only did he want to make this point to Ed, he also didn't want to

105

check out the competition with an entourage—you learn more from checking out your competition when you visit discreetly, something Fred has always made a point of doing.

Windshield Time and Other Key Learning Moments

Personally, I enjoyed spending time in the field with staff. On the road between store visits during what we would call "windshield time" was time well spent, and more valuable than any meeting or office conversation. I learned so much simply by observing what interested them, and their responses to various situations. This informal style proved to be very conducive to getting closer to individuals with whom you worked. It also allowed an opportunity to get to know the individual on a more personal basis. It was always interesting to see what interests they would have and how often it was similar to mine. As a young and impressionable executive growing up in the system, I was eager to learn, at every opportunity, always on the lookout to pick up cues from anyone, whether they were formal or not.

Lesson Learned

Achievers never stop learning. They absorb every facet of an organization, and as leaders we must nurture that, and never forget that we are role models, even when we least consider ourselves to be.

Field visits were learning experiences for everyone, agreed Tom Dentice, a retired executive vice president, who mentioned that "there was a lack of elitism, the feeling that none of us is as good as all of us. And so everyone in operations really did what it took to get the job done, and that's how we did it. Everybody understood that. The field managers, it just works all the way back to the crew. I was in a store one day, and I had been away from it for a while, and they got busy and I jumped on the grill. I was doing Big Mac's and I lost the center section . . . just lost them," Tom said, referring to the middle section of the bun. "And it's all over, and the crewman that was working with me said, 'You don't do this often do you?' and with that we all had a big laugh."

There was a lot to discover from observing those company executives as they conducted field visits. Mike Roberts, former president of McDonald's, and now a consultant in his own firm, mentioned to me an incident with Fred that he felt exemplified the spirit of leading by example. "I was managing a store in Naperville [Illinois], and I was there less than a month. Fred came in and visited with every crew person, every station in the restaurant. We looked at the managers' schedule, the crew schedule, we talked about local store marketing—it was terrific. . . . He ingrained in all of us, that *this is about the restaurant.* . . . Years later I am with another client, and I ask, do they ever meet any of their customers? Have they visited any of their facilities outside of this one? And the answer is no." It was that obsession with the smallest detail—evident throughout the system, and exemplified especially by top management—that set McDonald's apart from the rest.

Personally, I liked visiting stores. I tracked my office versus field time because I knew how important it was to be visible in the stores. I placed percentages of field time versus office time to keep a balance. It allowed me to maintain tabs with store managers and franchisees. I also tried to have as many meetings in different restaurants as possible. And by walking in for an unannounced visit, I'd get a real feel for a store's operations. If, for example, I'd walk in to the back room and find lights that were out, or not cleaned, it would indicate a sign of neglect that's likely accumulated over time. In addition, store managers were always very open to say what was going on, so I'd have a feel for the issues. These visits provided snapshots I wouldn't have seen sitting inside the office. In my own consulting today, I urge my clients to get out in the field, closest to the staff and the customers, and once they do, they agree, nothing provides greater insights and perspectives than on-site visits.

In fact, McDonald's valued field visits so much that it held an annual Founder's Day, where everyone in the entire company goes into the stores for a day. That tradition continues in a number of countries to this date.

On the corporate side, leading by example provided an edge: It gave you an insider's look as to what goes on in the stores, and it put you right there with the customers—invaluable when it came to making decisions for the system. In the early years, Gerry Newman, McDonald's chief accounting officer, understood that intuitively. He knew that by working side by side with regional managers and operators that they would not only ascertain his respect for them but also sense his support—an important quality when trying to win buy-in for initiatives within the system. He enjoyed getting into the stores and visiting them whenever he was in a region. He along with many other "support" officers from the Chicago office all seemed to relish their time in the field with us. They understood the power of getting close to the action and shoulder to shoulder with staff, customers, and suppliers. It provides a huge advantage in gaining a perspective on what is going on in the business. And McDonald's provided a culture that respected store visits.

Those working in corporate spoke with pride about the hours they spent in the store. I still remember sharing a taxi from the airport to the corporate office with a woman who worked in the accounting department. She was proud to tell me how she had pitched in on a weekend when an owner was short-staffed. This meant that her husband and children had to wait for her in the dining room to finish helping out! As an operations-based company, you earn your stripes behind the counter.

Lesson Learned

Build a culture where corporate staff members are encouraged to work in the field. In all likelihood, they will return to the office enthused, and with a new appreciation for the importance of the work field staff does on a daily basis.

Gerry Newman was the one executive operators turned to when they questioned new programs put forth by the system. And because he was not the kind of executive who stationed himself behind a desk, he was both approachable and resourceful. If an operator struggled with financing a newly required piece of equipment, Gerry would sit and figure out a way to show how a loan could be used as investment spending, say, $5,000 would result in additional revenues of $30,000. He took the time to demonstrate what was possible, and because he invested his time in the field, he built up the track record and credibility with the operators. What Gerry demonstrated to many of us in the field was the importance of the finance end of the system. Refinancing, watching overhead, and smart reinvestments that showed good returns as well as maintaining the profitability of each restaurant were shown over and over again.

"He dug in, and rolled up his sleeves, and tried to make a difference by getting in and dealing with the problems that had built up," Fred Turner noted, referring to Gerry. "He was a hands-on guy. He would drill down, and he learned. He learned from regional managers, he learned a little bit from me, and he was persuasive in getting the operators to act. He would be prepared to make decisions."

Money Talks

It's true. Sometimes you have to put your money where your mouth is, as Frank Behan recalled. One of the operators never changed the shortening in his fryers, and the situation was so bad that Frank, during a store visit, went to the filtering machine and dumped the vats. Upset, the operator threatened to call the police. "Go ahead and I'll turn you in to the health department," Frank said. Then the operator pled that he could not afford to replace the shortening, so Frank reached into his pocket and gave him $10 and said, "Here, replace it." That did the trick. "He never had a problem with that again," Frank said. Show them what practices you won't tolerate, and they'll get the message, loud and clear.

Not Always Fool-Proof

Of course, even the best leaders won't succeed every time. No matter how good a leader you are, you will run into your share of folks who won't follow your guidelines, regardless of how many models of excellence you put before them. The McDonald's system accounted for that too. "Everyone has that passion in common, and I think you were flushed quickly if you didn't, an incredibly strong work ethic," former McDonald's divisional president Debra Koenig noted.

A Backup Plan

Despite the system's propensity for leadership, the company had its flaws—as any company does. Take the company-operated stores, which were created to generate profits for the company and develop management for the system. Generally speaking, McDonald's worked hard to maintain a standard of excellence in the company stores. And yet there were instances when these stores were not run properly. They had a unique handicap: the lack of an on-premise entrepreneur—one of the key components of the three-legged stool. And even if they had great managers, those were the ones who got promoted quickly, so the consistency of management in those stores was always an issue. Many times these stores were sold to owner/operators who put in their full-time best efforts and therefore were more successful at pushing the sales and operation levels up to their full potential. If we could not lead by example, then we would sell them so they ran right. It also showed that as a company we put our words into actions. Selling these stores to franchisees was the ultimate backup plan.

Leading by Example: Additional Benefits

Lead by example and you not only will model expectations but also demonstrate the McDonald's career path for staff members, fostering company loyalty. This is evident everywhere at McDonald's. Currently, in fact:

- 33 percent of franchisees started out as crew.
- 42 percent of worldwide top management of the company started their careers by serving customers.
- 63.6 percent of company restaurant managers started as crew.
- 31.5 percent of operations and midmanagement level staff started as crew.
- 18.4 percent of nonrestaurant staff above administrative level started as crew.

In my tenure, the talented and capable rose through the ranks like a badge of honor, if that was their desire. Role models sent the message to crew that "you're going to get here, too." Of course, some were content with crew status. Stay-at-home moms, for instance, were happy to work only while their children were at school and weren't looking to step up the career ladder. And older workers were content to pick up the extra cash to supplement their retirement income, but had no aspirations for anything further. And that was okay. McDonald's had a place for them, knowing they would add value to the system because role models who demonstrated expectations applied to them, too.

This early encouragement of climbing the promotional ladder demonstrated the possibilities of a career path. While it has been mentioned previously about the highly tenured management ranks within McDonald's, as well as the ability to promote executive level talent, the value behind this strategy is now substantiated by objective analysis. In the book *Good to Great*, Jim Collins mentions a survey of the best companies, writing: "Ten out of eleven good to great CEO's came from *inside* the company. The comparison companies turned to outsiders with *six times* greater frequency—yet they failed to produce sustained great results."

Giving Back

McDonald's has long valued giving back to the community, a practice that dates back to the 1950s. The system's charitable efforts were rewarded by publicity in the local press, which went a long way toward branding. But it would be cynical to say that was the only upside. As Ray Kroc put it in *Grinding It Out*, "I don't make charitable donations because they will give me tax deductions. . . . I have always enjoyed helping other people . . . and I take genuine pleasure in sharing my good fortune with others." Putting his money where his mouth is, Ray started the Kroc Foundation, which provided luxurious customized buses complete with kitchens, restrooms, phones, and color televisions to take disadvantaged children and senior citizens on outings. The foundation also supported research into diabetes, multiple sclerosis, and arthritis as well as raised awareness about alcohol abuse. But that wasn't all. The foundation also supported cultural institutions, hospitals, universities, and even prison rehabilitative programs.

Recipients were put on Ray's "birthday list." "When I added it all up, my birthday gift list totaled seven and a half million dollars. I'll tell you, it felt mighty good to be able to announce that kind of present!" Ray wrote in *Grinding It Out*.

Following Ray's lead, the company itself continued the tradition of giving back, sponsoring high school bands in the Macy's Thanksgiving Day Parade, the McDonald's All-American Games that features all-star basketball athletes, and the Ronald McDonald House Charities. Ray had wanted all franchisees to give back to the communities in which they lived, and demonstrated that by his giving, which helped to proliferate the tradition ever since.

The momentum permeated corporate as well. Fred Turner encouraged me to get out and involved in other activities within the New York area when I was regional vice president. We were never represented by previous management on any associations or boards within the market. I asked one of the leading operators to help me find out who was running the New York Urban League. I had watched McDonald's nationally in its involvement with this group, and following the company's lead, was drawn by their motto of "equal opportunity." Who could not support that concept? I thought that personified what McDonald's was to both operators and staff—the company provided opportunities regardless of race, gender, or age, and you had to run with it. I understood that everyone doesn't start on an equal playing field either. I went ahead and went through the interview process and became a board member shortly thereafter. Being new to such an influential group, and not knowing anyone, it was fairly intimidating at first. My fellow board members included numerous lawyers, judges, and political appointees as well as renowned New Yorkers—the kind you read about in the pages of the *New York Times*. It was an eclectic and interesting group. I quickly found that I was welcomed and that my energy and interest were appreciated, and the insights I garnered in my time with that organization have been instrumental in helping me understand and achieve balance in my business perspective. I stayed more than 20 years with the board, even well after I left McDonald's, and was proud to serve in various capacities including chairman for three of those years.

In Summary

At McDonald's, no task was too small for even the top executives. They relished being in the field and getting up close to the customer. Their passion is contagious, and has spurred the rest of us to share that same enthusiasm. Leading by example, they demonstrated the importance of QSC to everyone in the system. When leaders live and breathe the organization's missions and values, they inspire everyone else to impart those same ideals, pushing everyone to accomplish more together as a group.

Key Learnings

✔ Demonstrate model behaviors. The essence of leading by example is exhibiting a participatory style of involvement, showing that no task is too humble, even for the boss. It is the leadership's actions that set in motion the behaviors and values of the organization. Your staff will find your involvement and commitment both encouraging and motivating.

✔ Become customer driven. The closer you are to the customer, and the employees who service the customer directly, the more you will benefit by being close to the action. Observe, mentor, show, praise, correct, and communicate when out of the office environment.

✔ Never underestimate your actions. Staff at all levels is constantly picking up on management's cues. Turn this into an opportunity to coach employees. Your access and visibility will give you a great occasion to show commitment to your employees and remove barriers to their achievement of company goals.

✔ Turn field visits into teaching moments so that associates will gain an appreciation for qualities your organization values as well as areas that require improvement.

✔ Use field visits as an opportunity to understand what goes on at the lowest levels. This approach provides a surefire method for understanding operations systemwide, both in what is working as well as what can be improved.

✔ Highlight the career path at your organization. Demonstrate how those who live and breathe your mission and values find new opportunities for growth. This is an excellent strategy for retaining talent. Show the opportunities.

✔ Establish meaningful philanthropic roots in the community. Stakeholders will appreciate your efforts in making their world a better place, and will value the importance of "giving back."

5 Courage:
Telling It Like It Is

Achievement must be made against the possibility of failure, against the risk of defeat. It is no achievement to walk a tightrope that is stretched flat on the floor . . . or to win at tennis without a net. Where there is no risk, there is no achievement and where there is no achievement, there is no real happiness.

—Ray Kroc

McDonald's has never taken the easy out. When Ray first began to franchise the company, he wanted to grow the company sustainably, even if it meant turning down fast money. Rather than sell territories to investors for some quick cash, he held out for individuals in whose interest it would serve to nurture each unit so it would flourish. "You make the first dollar, we'll make the second" was Ray's motto. He also made the decision early on that he would not make money from selling his licensee's products, which was the normal practice back in the 1950s when franchising first took off. It takes courage to start and grow a business, but perhaps it takes even more courage to walk away from opportunity—especially when an audience is expecting you to do one thing and you decide to do another.

Yet Fred Turner did just that back in the late 1980s, when he turned down a staggeringly lucrative deal—hundreds of millions of dollars—positioning McDonald's on all of the U.S. Army bases. Over the course of many months, individuals within the corporation as well as within the Army worked on the deal, and it was the first of its kind anywhere. The real estate and legal people had worked long and hard to put this together, and the publicity and marketing aspects presented tremendous opportunity. In the end, it boiled down to Fred signing off on the deal. Yet Fred was never known to bow to pressure.

In fact, Fred was troubled about the deal. As he saw it, there was something largely missing in the equation—namely, the franchisee. These stores were to be Army-run post exchanges, with the Army as the franchisee—and at such a large scale it was critical that they be run right. And the fact that the company was based on individuals running their restaurants on a daily basis, with personal hands-on involvement, Fred sensed that the best efforts would not be put into the venture. The matter required more consideration. In the end, Fred killed the deal and walked away, much to the surprise and concern of everyone involved. He was not going to sacrifice the enduring principles of licensing that had nurtured the system for so many years. Recalling that episode, Fred told me: "The U.S. Army, McDonald's—you need a proprietor, you need the owner, that's our system. And I stuck with that, and since then, there has been some compromise on that. But even now, when you're forced to have a corporate franchisee you could have an operating partner and he would have a percentage of the business and incentives. Or have the same incentive as an owner/operator has. So what I did for the Army has become the model for others."

The decision took guts, and I wonder how many chief executives of a public corporation would have Fred's gumption or his insight. There's one thing for sure, courage comes with a strong identity—knowing who you are and what you stand for. As Fred put it: "It was huge. . . . I was sweating bullets; it was a hard decision. I knew we'd find a way later on to get in. We had to stick to our formula—had to stick with who we are and how we do things. And we face this decision all over the world; now as we expand and get into other countries we're going to face it more and more."

> ### Lesson Learned
>
> Walk away from deals that don't feel right, no matter how much time was invested or how much money you might stand to gain. Trust your instincts, and put your energy to more favorable opportunities instead. As the saying goes, "You need to know when to get off the train."

119

Courage as a Legacy

Fred's prediction proved correct, and the heirs to his legacy showed the same boldness. CEO Jim Skinner related a story of similar circumstances when looking for the best possible franchisees in Latin America: "We had a decision to make in Latin America for licensing. We had other choices, and could have gone with a more heavily financed individual, but we would have violated the system by doing that. We are sticking to our values, and Ralph [Alvarez, chief operations officer] and I both thought about it overnight, and we went with the right person in the right place at the right time. He was committed to the people in his organization and committed to the system. And those decisions take courage."

Back in January 2003, when Jim Cantalupo took over the reigns as CEO of McDonald's, he inherited a company that had suffered several quarters of poor sales. And when Wall Street is not happy, the pressures on a CEO to quickly improve performance are enormous. The market reads every movement, every decision, with an eye toward getting a clue on a possible swing of financial fortunes. Instead of heeding what many CEOs would do in such a case, which is to boost up new-store growth to show immediate sales gain, Jim did the opposite. He announced that he would *cut* the development of new stores, and focus on getting more sales in existing restaurants. As Jeff Stratton, chief restaurant officer, said to me of this era, "He returned the focus of our business to the core." Mike Roberts, president of U.S. operations at the time, described Jim's actions this way: "It took extraordinary courage, in my mind, for him to support the U.S. agenda at the time. We had to go to Wall Street and get our primary investors aligned."

Additionally, Jim proposed an incentive to operators who would take profit dollars from the corporation to help the operators pay for the "reimaging" plan to enhance the stores' look to the customers. It hardly seemed a remedy for a jilted stock price. He instinctively knew his strategy was right for the system—it was a return to some of the basic principles he had grown up with and witnessed, and it would bear fruit later on. That took courage, both of his convictions and to endure the outcry from his detractors.

Jack Welch, former chairman and CEO of General Electric, in an April 2008 *BusinessWeek* article had this to say about courage: "It's the one behavior bureaucrats shun and too many managers avoid."

Breaking from the Status Quo

Courage. It may seem like an unlikely principle within a corporate culture, but as I witnessed, it was a component within the system on all levels. And the culture of courage at McDonald's started with Ray, who was known to say, "Success is not free. Neither is failure."

Fred told me that "Ray loved risk takers—people who had the courage of their convictions who took the initiatives. I took on projects even if they flopped. And I always felt bad, and he'd say to me, 'Well, Fred, that's why they put mats under cuspidors,'" Fred said, referring to what was also known as a spittoon in earlier days.

And so we were all encouraged to take risks. Maybe we were so grounded by the standards of McDonald's that we knew when to reach—because we all did it, in both big ways and small. We pulled from within ourselves to navigate whenever we found ourselves in predicaments that weren't covered in the manual. And on the restaurant floor, there are times when you find yourself without a script. You certainly can't script human behaviors. The crew and your customers look to you for direction—so you had better be ready to take a stand.

121

Although it helped to look to the system's standards, you needed a certain amount of guts to push for what was right, especially when breaking from the status quo. For example, when I first took over as regional manager in 1988, there had been seven new owner/operators in the last seven years in the entire region. True, there was an average of one new operator per year, but these were all next generation—sons and daughters of current franchisees. I thought the system would benefit with an infusion of new blood. I wanted to bring into the system individuals who had success in other areas and could enhance and challenge the group. And with such a diverse population as New York, it only made sense to embrace the idea of diversity within the operator ranks. They were part of the community, and our customers, and if they had the right skills, and the passion, they would thrive personally, as would the restaurants. This was the direction I was introducing, and it upset some of the established owners, who feared that additional franchisees would mean they'd have less of the pie. But I ran with the concept. I added six new operators in 1988, nine in 1989, and 13 in 1990. Of the 28 new operators, four were Hispanic, five were African American, five were women, and one was Chinese. This rocked the status quo on a regional level, but I was picking up on the corporate lead, and I didn't back down. In my conference room, I kept as a reminder a plaque upon which is inscribed Niccolo Machiavelli's famous words:

There is nothing more difficult to take in hand, more perilous to conduct, or more uncertain in its success, than to take the lead in the introduction of a new order of things.

Change is never easy, and this incident was no different. To me, diversity made sense; it was an extension of the culture of opportunity in McDonald's. I wanted to make a difference by setting new policy in the region, and it figured into our growth, which over the next few years kept us in the top three regions nationally. In the end, the courage to carry out what I thought was right brought outstanding results. And the operators were great in helping and welcoming the new franchisees. They understood after the initial introduction that these were some really talented individuals with the same aspirations as they had years back. The new group of operators became a much better model of the population they served.

Courage figured into every decision, including which operator qualified for expansion and which did not—decisions that literally meant millions of dollars in revenues for franchisees—and the outcome often emotionally affected those who were denied. Some were politically connected, and yes, they'd go ballistic when told they didn't qualify this time around. Having standards and metrics gave me the objective tools I needed to make the right decisions and, in working with the staff, the courage to believe in my convictions.

Owners, too, showed courage. It's easy to dismiss this today, as the brand is so successful, but one has to understand what during those early years individuals were giving up to change careers. In the book *Behind the Arches*, John F. Love writes about "franchisees that set a pattern for the type of operator on which Kroc would build McDonald's. They were giving up jobs in other careers, risking on McDonald's all their savings and, typically, all the money they could borrow from friends and relatives."

While a good number rose through the system and had a sense of what they were getting into, others did not, risking everything for the chance to be an entrepreneur within the McDonald's system. Take Sam Samaha, an owner/operator since 1973. "I was 45 when I started," Sam told me. "I had a good job and I left to buy a McDonald's, and my wife said, 'What the hell are we doing?' I was leaving a job with a good corporation and ongoing into something completely unknown. But I think you have to have a sense of wanting to have your own business. Entrepreneurship. I knew my limitations; I think you have to put that along with courage and be willing to invest your time as well as money and take a chance, which in this case worked out very well."

As a McDonald's veteran owner/operator for the last 19 years, with six restaurants, Ron Bailey stated, "I think as a franchisee, leaving a career and leaving what was a great job to follow a vision—and that vision was an opportunity—offered to me a chance where I can step out of the box. And stepping out of the box, especially as an African American, I was limited in terms of what I could do. We both have to have courage: McDonald's to have faith in me, and me to venture out, and not just venturing out in the neighborhood, but going clear across the country to an unknown area."

123

Vendors, too, showed courage, as pointed out by Frank Kuchuris, a second-generation baker of buns whose father, Louie Kuchuris, built an 87,000-square-foot plant in 1967 to better serve McDonald's, all based on a handshake. While this may sound foolhardy, Louie, a supplier since 1955, knew the system and its standards and its leaders—an equation in which he had great faith, and he was proved right, as the company is now one of the largest suppliers of buns in the system worldwide, covering 14 countries, along with the United States.

Peter Grimm, also a long-time bun supplier, shared his thoughts on courage as it played out in McDonald's initial history: "It took courage to do the right thing, even when no one was looking. And don't forget, in the early years there weren't that many people looking."

Because we saw so many examples of courage around us, we didn't back down. As former McDonald's executive Debra Koenig said: "It would have been easier as a corporate executive to not take on the tough challenges, one could just close your eyes, sort of ignore it, and life would have been easier. That isn't the culture we grew up in. We grew up to protect the brand, recognize the standards, and take on the challenges."

With courage fitting into the corporate equation, we grew up in the system as young decision makers, and I'd argue that today most of us look back at the calls we made and say on average, we did okay. As former CEO Mike Quinlan put it, "When I was a young field consultant, and then a field service manager, and supervisor, I had some difficult decisions to make during those times. And I never took the easy way and, boy, am I glad."

Fighting the Good Fight

That quest to take on the challenges is what emboldened me as a 19-year-old night manager to break up a fight between two rivaling motorcycle gangs displaying their colors at a Long Island McDonald's parking lot one summer night. At least, that's the best motive to which I now relate my actions.

Upon hearing the ruckus, I looked out the window and started getting the sinking feeling that I, the manager on duty, would have to confront these guys sooner rather than later. Out of the corner of my eye, I saw food being thrown around and one guy pushing and punching in half jest, but clearly it was getting out of hand.

This was bad for our customers, and I knew it was my responsibility to take control. But how? It wasn't like I could look up the solution in the manual. If I called the cops, would they say that the gangs really weren't doing anything warranting police action? That would just tick off the gangs. And, at the time, managers on the floor wore a distinctive red hat signifying "manager," so the two gangs would clearly know who called. More to the point, there were 12 to 15 of them and only one of me . . . and I was all of 5 feet, 8 inches and probably 150 pounds at the time. What match is that?

Food began to fly, hitting the windows and making a general mess of the lot and seating area outside, and I knew my time had come. I had to go out there and face the consequences. I let my crew—who by this time was a bit nervous about what might happen to them and our store, let alone me—know that if things got bad out there, call the cops. Right away. Out I went, in my best "*High Noon* walk," to face my adversaries.

Despite their jeers, I approached the burliest one in the bunch. "Listen," I said, somehow not stammering. "I am the one responsible for this restaurant, and I can't let you guys make a mess here and fight. It's a family atmosphere here, and I'll have to call the cops if you continue. Why don't you guys go across the street, and you can do all you want [it was an empty shopping center lot]. I get to keep my job, and you guys get to hang out without anyone bothering you."

125

I made my way back inside, unscathed but no doubt flushed with fright, and clueless to what the outcome would be, and told the crew, who'd been glued to the window, to get back to work. Suddenly, we heard the racket of screeching tires and smelled rubber burning as the last of the bikes left. I walked out the door, and started to clean up some of the mess they left, looking up the road to discover that they had actually done what I suggested and set up in the empty lot across the street. Back then, I wasn't sure how I had the courage to take on not just one gang, but two. Yet now I see that I summoned up everything the system had taught me about treating everyone with the same degree of respect, regardless of age, gender, even appearance, to stand up for the brand, and never stop thinking about protecting the customer experience. And as a backup, instruct the crew to be prepared to call the cops. Breaking up gang fights wasn't covered in the manual, but somehow the system still taught me what to do. I know this scenario is not unusual—it has played out thousands of times by managers within the system over the years.

In fact, courage at the crew level is pervasive. As Roland Jones describes in his book, *Standing Up & Standing Out*, one crew member, disturbed that an associate had written and left racist notes in a soon-to-be-opened Tennessee store, stood up after a motivational meeting and said "to the person who wrote this . . . we don't want you on our team and we wish you'd resign now." According to Roland, the rest of the crew gave her a standing ovation, and consequently two male workers never showed up again. It also demonstrated that the social unit of the crew, when operating as a truly engaged team, will do much to self-police their own actions.

In deploying his street smarts, Roland also managed to stop crime in his Nashville store, which had been the scene of several armed robberies. He placed a police radio monitor out of view, with the volume set just loud enough to suggest that police were actually in the store. He also befriended police officers, inviting them to speak at team meetings, increasing their presence at the store. And he taught his crew to greet and observe customers the moment they entered the store—an approach he thinks deterred would-be criminals from striking. As Roland demonstrated, it was important to fight crime, but equally critical to do so with some out-of-the-box deterrents.

Troubling as some of these experiences seem, they also help you develop a tough exterior. I know it helped me overcome other episodes during my career, including personal threats and even a shotgun in my chest during a holdup.

Lesson Learned

As leaders, we find that people turn to us to diffuse potential or actual altercations. So use your smarts—especially when it comes to personal safety. Developing a plan of action to deter crime is a critical first step.

You had to be tough to persevere over that kind of element, and sometimes that tough element actually existed within the system, as former CEO Mike Quinlan reminded me, when he shared a story about serving as the new regional manager after being the district manager for only seven months in St. Louis. Now, here he was in Washington, D.C., his new region. It was the early 1970s, and this region had its share of troubles. In particular, Mike learned from his predecessor about five licensees who ran poor operations. "I thought to myself: I'm not going to spend my life out here pandering to the bad guys and trying to reform them, because if I spend my time doing that, when do I get the good stuff done? So I got in my car and I got on a plane and I went to all five of these bad guys. . . . And I basically looked them in the eye, each one of them, and I said, 'It's over.' Now, I am 28 years old as a regional manager, I said, 'It's over. You're done.'" They tried to place blame on Mike's predecessor, but Mike stood tough. "I said, 'No, No. It's over. So, here's how it's going to be. I will offer to buy you out, within a week, I will give you a fair price, I will give you a check. If you don't accept my offer, I will be all over you. Now, do you want it the nice way or the bad way? I'll call Kroc. Pick up the phone, right now. Let's go.' One of them took me up on it. He regretted that. And Kroc called me up personally, and says, 'It's about time someone got that son of a bitch.' The right thing was to look this guy in the eye and say, 'You are going, I'll give you a chance. Don't think that I don't mean it. Don't make that mistake.' And you know what? I went five for five. Didn't waste a lot of time on it either."

For Mike, it paid off. "It took me two-and-a-half years, and then, we were number one in everything," he said. "Sales, openings, percentage rent, and profit. The whole run. The reason, though, was that I had courage. Maybe I was ignorant and didn't know any better; looking back, I think that there was some of that in there."

I'm not sure that kind of approach would still be effective in today's corporate environment, but at the time, it took courage for Mike to take such a position with owner/operators who did not meet the standards—and Mike's stance was part of the style back then. And you can be sure his operators listened well to him from that point onward.

The Courage to Admit You're Wrong

That culture of courage bred a system where those with determination weren't afraid to fight for what they believed in. Sure, there were heated battles, and yes, they were uncomfortable sometimes, but in the end those who spoke up were respected for it. Irv Klein, a retired multiple operator, remembered the courage it took as Operators National Advertising Board (OPNAD) chairman to stand up for the other operators during one of their meetings. They were upset with Fred Turner, who wanted permission to advertise a 99-cent Egg McMuffin on national television. Concerned about advertising expenses, the operators were opposed to it. "Fred came to me, and said, 'Irv, I want you to do it for me,'" Irv recalled. "I said to him, 'The operators voted not to do it.' And he said to me, 'Mr. Klein, I want you to do it for me.' And I said to him, 'I went from Irv to Mr. Klein—how does that work?' He said, 'Because I'm telling you I really want this.' And of course, there was a guy in the back of the room who got up and said, 'I think we ought to "do it for Fred."' I was so annoyed at that point and I said to him, 'That isn't what you said to me out in the hall 15 minutes ago; it was, "Irv, go get 'em," remember?' Finally, Fred got up and said the corporation would pay for the ad so that the operators would not have to fund it. Later, Fred returned to an afternoon session and said, 'Irv and I don't always agree, but he was right on this one. So he's right once in a while.'"

Lesson Learned

People will respect you for having the courage to admit when you're wrong. Adding a dose of humor to the admission may make it easier to smooth things over and move on.

Fred wasn't afraid to admit when he was wrong. And Irv might have tangled himself with politics, but instead he fought for what he was certain was right. Most of us would not have expected him to do anything less in such a culture.

Courage often has a by-product: ego. But when it came to protecting the brand, ego took a second seat. This was obvious when Fred conceded to Irv, and it was not an anomaly. Fred reminded me of an episode in 1976, when McDonald's was rolling out the Egg McMuffin, and the product wasn't selling to its potential. Ed Schmitt, the president of McDonald's at the time, felt it prudent to market it on national television but Fred—who felt it was premature to run the campaign—was out of the country. So Ed made the decision in Fred's absence. "He was convinced he was right, and that I was wrong in not wanting to do it," Fred recalled. "And he knew that I wouldn't like that, that I would feel that's premature and we need more time. Ed was right and I was wrong. I acknowledge I was wrong, and I commend Ed for the guts to go along and do it."

The Guts to Make a Personal Commitment

In discussing the principle of courage with Tom Dentice, retired executive vice president, he smiled when recalling an incident that transpired just as he was about to retire. It was extremely controversial at the time, and took a tremendous amount of courage to stay the course. "I had been working with the BMOA [Black McDonald's Operators Association] for some time in my role and they had concerns . . . over their ability to grow, and if they would be given a fair share. For years we had been trying to move them along, and we were making progress, but it certainly wasn't at light speed. And we met with a group of them. The operators that really did well and did a good job were savvy and knew what was going on. They presented their case over a couple of days about how we had been promising them progress and kept falling short." Later that evening, Tom went home, consumed about the events of the meeting. He wrote a letter that night, supporting the BMOA's goals and making a commitment to meet specific goals within five years. Then Tom considered his options. "I said, 'Well, I could do one of three things with this letter when I re-read it. I [could] take it to the [executive] management team; I could take it to the president; I could take it to the CEO.' But if I do that, it isn't going to say what it says now when I'm done. It will get watered down." Ultimately, Tom decided to send the letter as is. "This was a personal commitment, and it was a personal commitment letter," Tom noted. "I didn't say *McDonald's Corporation* will. . . . I said *I* would make sure that things happen." The letter triggered controversy, but Tom kept his stance. "Everyone felt we were making a commitment that couldn't be met and we overstepped what we could accomplish," Tom said. "I had a plan. I knew what it was going to take before I wrote the letter. I knew the commitment." When I asked Tom how it resolved, he said, "I was retired, and I got a call from the head of minority operations, Ray Mines, and he said, just simply . . . we did it. It got done."

131

Alone in a Crowd

The company perpetuated a culture of risk taking, of "telling it like it is." And no one ever got fired for taking a risk—an important detail behind McDonald's accomplishments. As Ray Kroc said, "You'll become successful and happy when you plan something and the necessary risks. If your plans don't work out, try something new." I saw early on at McDonald's that avoiding risks, skirting and being indecisive, were hardly tolerated. Because we were encouraged to challenge, and the results at the end were never harmful or had repercussions, we engaged in such activity. Still, not everyone felt as I did, and I never quite understood later in situations why many of my peers would not speak up if they had a difference of opinion. I believe that it helped me get to know the leadership of the organization on a much better level, years later. In one memorable episode, I was a department head in a room of my peers at a national conference for operations. More than 200 people were present and chairman of the board Mike Quinlan was making a case for changing the grading policy of the restaurants. This was always a controversial topic. As he wound down his rationale, and asked for any thoughts, I instinctively put my hand up to question the wisdom of what he was suggesting. I thought, incorrectly, that my group around me, who were clearly not in favor of the change and whispering as much in the audience, would have their hands up as well. Not. I realized as I looked around the room that I had the only hand up! Not a good feeling.

Now it was me and the chairman of the board, mano a mano. I quickly summarized my points as best I could, making the case how it would adversely affect operations and not allow the stores to measure themselves. Mike was cordial and thanked me for my comments in front of the audience. Although grading went through as presented, within two years it was back again. I discovered that while you could question, you had to do it in the right way. Have the courage to speak up, but present your arguments in a professional, objective manner. Conflict was good, but don't take it personally. Surprisingly to me, not everyone spoke up the way I and others did, but I believe I was availed with more opportunities because I spoke my mind. In fact when I retired, then-president Alan Feldman said, "Now that Paul is stepping down, who is going to challenge us?" I took that as a compliment.

Lesson Learned

Have the courage to speak up calmly and in an organized fashion to present your perspective, even if it seems to go against the grain of your higher-ups. Leaders of well-run organizations will usually respect your point of view.

One on One with Mike Quinlan, former CEO

The system thrived on straight shooters. Mike Quinlan was no exception. I spoke with Mike at his home in Chicago about the courage required in leadership. "If you tell the truth and you deal straight with people, and that means the bad as well as the good, you will probably get to the right point," Mike told me. "Now you have to temper that with political realities, and that's a learned skill."

But as Mike pointed out, though it's a difficult skill to learn it's important to do the right thing, even though that road is a tough one. "It is always easier to take the easy way, the expedient way," Mike pointed out. "Give the C-operator the store, shut him up, avoid the conflict, look the other way. Let a supplier slide, look the other way when somebody isn't quite getting the job done instead of calling it right there."

Mike noted: "Unfortunately you learn by experience that the expedient way and the easy way in the long run is not the right way. But you have to take a lot of things into consideration to determine that."

And one of the necessary traits needed is courage. "Those don't have courage in the long run will fail," Mike said. Still, "sometimes in the short run they won't fail, they do the popular thing."

A Safe Place to Take Risks

Claire Babrowski, a former executive vice president, recalled a decision she made as regional manager when serving in Raleigh, North Carolina. "We needed to compete in our marketplace, and fresh-made biscuits, I knew, I could do better locally," she said. So she went on to push for a local supplier, even though the corporation was working on its version. She did it on her own. She pushed and went ahead and introduced them to the stores, and the biscuits became a staple on the menu and proved to be very successful. She demonstrated what Ed Rensi liked to say, as president of the company: "Ask for forgiveness, not permission." Breaking out of the box of convention, she did what she felt was right for her region, and it worked. She didn't need to ask for forgiveness. Risk, courage—these traits were supported at McDonald's.

So, too, going to bat for someone was supported, if you had trust in that person's judgment. This worked to my advantage as a regional vice president, when, during an austerity budget, I wanted to hire an individual who I knew would be a great fit for us. But I also knew that we definitely didn't have the budget to add another employee. Still, zone manager Rob Doran, my boss at the time, said, "Do it," much to my surprise. He trusted my instincts and knew that I would not go to him with such a request unless it was very important. Because he trusted in me, he was willing to take the heat from his boss, at the time the president of the company, knowing in the long run that hiring this person was the right thing to do. That hire proved to be valuable well beyond my expectations.

Yet not everyone was necessarily eager to be the first to take an issue and run with it. Many sat back. As Willis Smart pointed out to me, "Many solidified their way to success by staying underneath the radar and finding ways to accommodate, and not make waves. The fact was that taking on the tough issues was something that you plan in advance, and you know that it is not going to be easy."

Still, the freedom to experiment, often with baby steps, was alive and well. Bob Weissmueller, retired division vice president and former CEO of Fazolis, recalled an encounter with Fred regarding a new building experiment—an initiative that Bob's bosses had recently canceled because they did not support the project. Bob felt that decision was shortsighted. He expressed his frustration at a convention weeks later, in a casual conversation with Fred. At the last day of the convention, Fred walked up to Bob and said, "I want you to go ahead and build some more. Keep me abreast. Let's see how this goes—and don't go crazy." Fred gave his permission to keep going, albeit under the radar, against the verdict of Bob's immediate bosses. So we had the ability to get beyond some barricades and help others see the big picture as we knew it. We were allowed to take risks and encouraged to do so.

Food for Thought
How Can You Encourage Risk Taking in Your Own Organization?

Welcome new ideas from your associates but challenge them to think through every step of their plan. This way, only the carefully strategized plans will win approval.

Don't condemn those risk takers who do fail. Instead, consider it a learning experience—and the price of grooming loyal employees who may just bring your organization the next big idea. Don't waste time and energy on blame games.

"If you made the wrong decision, nobody came in and beat the hell out of you for it, or fired you for it, or called you stupid," noted Tom Dentice. "Nobody played the blame game. They just said, 'Well, Tom, you sure learned something from that one, right?' And you didn't make the same mistake twice."

In *Behind the Arches*, John F. Love states, "The key ingredient in Kroc's management formula is a willingness to risk failure and to admit mistakes." That has clearly imbedded itself into the culture of the organization.

On a Humane Level

If you're going to be a straight shooter, you've got to tell it like it is—not just to the upper echelons of the organization but also to those who report to you. And at times, this could get awkward, as I discovered as a 22-year-old store manager when I recognized that one of my assistant managers had a problem whose existence he did not acknowledge. Or, maybe he did not even realize it. But I knew the outcome could be potentially embarrassing. This manager, a good all-around guy and well liked by the crew, had a very bad case of body odor. Leaving soap bars on his desk and subtly asking about the kind of deodorant he used were to no avail. He just didn't get it. What's more, he unwittingly defied the fastidious values of Ray Kroc. I couldn't let it go.

While other organizations often have human resources departments to navigate such situations, I had no such support. As the store manager, the buck stopped at me—the assistant managers looked to me to fix it. It bothered me that the crew poked fun of this individual behind his back. How would I handle this?

I finally summed up the courage, having some bullet points that I would hit him with, by taking him one on one and letting him know how valuable he was to our team and how proud I was of working with him as he developed into a potential store manager.

After establishing this initial dialogue to build trust, I let him know that as both his friend and his boss I had an obligation to tell him things that perhaps no one else would. After that lead-in, I told him that, although he might not realize it, many were offended by his body odor. Maybe he could add extra bathing times or a better deodorant, I suggested. After expressing some shock initially, then moving to embarrassment, he was heartfelt in his appreciation that I told him. He took care of the situation. I learned a lot about developing your staff around you, and how honesty and being forthright with people is always the best way.

As author Bob Wall states in "Being Smart Only Takes You So Far," an article published in the June 2007 issue of *Training and Development*: "Leaders must also develop the courage to have difficult conversations. I've often heard employees complain that management fails to intervene when some are not performing well. This leads them to conclude that their managers don't notice poor performance or, worse yet, that they notice but don't care." I can't tell you how many conversations I have had with individuals who are distraught over the thought of a difficult conversation with one of their staff. I always try to remind them that as a leader it is your responsibility to coach your people, and you cannot do that without frank, honest, and insightful feedback. You must be committed to this and take action no matter how uncomfortable it may feel.

Lesson Learned

A true leader is able to be honest with his or her group and is strong enough to say what others might not. Your primary role as a leader is to develop your staff. It takes courage to make the right calls . . . and if you don't give honest feedback, then who will?

Steadfast and Focused

Like Ray and Fred, and like all of us in the system, you needed that strong identity to have the courage to do the job you set out to do, as Mike Quinlan reminded me. "People sometimes used to accuse me of pandering to the shareholders' stock price," he said. "That was unfair, but I knew down deep that at the end of the day it was my job to maximize the long-term returns of the shareholders. Now, there are a lot of things that need to get done to accomplish that: the operators needed opportunities to grow; suppliers have to get a raise. Nobody wants to work in an atmosphere where they aren't rewarded for their efforts. They have to see the opportunity to get a raise, to get a promotion. At the end of the day, you can only serve one guy . . ."

But in keeping Wall Street and investors happy, we had to keep our eye on the customer. In corporate, the customer wasn't only the consumers ordering burgers and fries, it was also the owner/operators. Our primary goal was to support them in their efforts to serve consumers. They valued that face time with corporate, and as a regional manager, at times that got difficult—even when it came to standing up to the higher-ups. On one occasion, when Ed Rensi, then the president of the company, came to visit New York, I arranged for a tour of stores and operators that spanned a full day, with a dinner that night as well. Tours were tough to coordinate, particularly with the president—you never knew how much time he was going to spend in each store. And no one was better than Ed at taking the time to talk with the crews and management of every store we visited. So it was up to me to keep to the tour schedule, which often meant cutting a visit short. The one thing you wanted to avoid was missing an appointment if a visit was planned; that would devastate the crew, management team, and operator. The chance to have the president of the company visit their store meant a great deal to everyone involved. Besides the normal bragging rights a visit allowed them, they valued the attention and ability to have one on one with the executives in their stores.

As usual, we ran a bit behind this day. I drove with Ed in the passenger seat and the field service manager and the director of operations in back. As we left a store in Brooklyn, Ed turned to me and said, "I feel like stopping for a good hot dog." This out-of-the-blue comment was not so unusual, as many times during tours we visited places of interest, including checking out the competition. But I was running out of time. I responded that Coney Island, the home of Nathan's, had the best hot dog. To which he responded, "Let's go."

Now I was at a crossroads. What do I do? Keep him happy and go get a hot dog, but disappoint one of the restaurants we were to visit? Or tell him no—to which he could certainly react in any number of ways to me?

I did what I thought was best, which was of course, to keep focused on the tour and forget the hot dog. I told him, "We can't go. We will be late for the other stores." As these words came out of my mouth, I watched the two guys in the back slink down in their seats, not believing what I just said and what might next happen.

Ed glared at me, but thankfully, didn't say anything the rest of the day about it. I assumed that I was not on Ed's favorite list that day. That night, after dinner, Ed turned to me and said, "You were right, I was wrong today. Glad you stayed with the agenda." Again. An acknowledgment that challenging was okay, at all levels.

In Summary

Courage has played a big role in McDonald's growth. From C-level to crew, individuals have shown the gumption to speak their mind and to fight for what they believe in. Many acknowl-

139

edge that there are times when it would be easy to look the other way, but somehow the culture taught us not to shirk challenges. While risk taking was encouraged, we were also expected to have our facts and numbers straight so that we stood on solid ground while venturing forward. Those with courage were respected, and their opinions were sought after. Organizations that foster courage, tempered with facts, stand to gain big wins.

Key Learnings

✔ Walk away from those deals you know in your gut are not right for your organization—no matter how much money is at stake. Be true to your principles.

✔ Encourage risk taking. In all likelihood, you won't achieve anything by playing it safe all of the time. But make it an educated, well-thought-out risk.

✔ Push for what is right—even if you're upsetting the status quo.

✔ Take on the challenges rather than pretending they don't exist. Courage is demonstrated through repetition in navigating tough challenges as they arise again and again.

✔ Speak your mind, respectfully. Others will appreciate you telling it like it is, and hopefully it will encourage others to speak up, too.

6 Communications

It's not how often you communicate,
but how well.

—Ray Kroc

Every company has its story to tell. And during my tenure at McDonald's, that company was no different. From its very beginning, Ray was mindful of McDonald's narrative, from the 15-cent hamburger to QSC, whether he was communicating internally to the regions, staff, franchisees, and vendors, or externally to the public or shareholders.

"It is essential that a strategic leader communicate his goals and objectives," Ed Rensi, former president of McDonald's, told me. "Strategic leaders have to have beliefs and values. They have to have a mission statement. You have to state your beliefs, values, and who you are. And when confronted with any decision, you have to go back and say where does it fit in your beliefs, where does it fit in your values, and where does it fit in with who you are. And if you can't get it to fit into all three categories, and it doesn't fit in your mission statement, then you're in trouble. I'm sure that neither Fred nor Ray was ever schooled at that. I'm equally sure that they understood it. One of the things about who we are is that we practice what is in the mission statement."

McDonald's ability to recognize the importance of communications steered the company through both good times, when company stakeholders had cause to celebrate over some great gain, and bad times, when the executive team strove to keep spirits high.

Decentralization

In McDonald's pervasive "never be satisfied" spirit, the company always sought improvements, and that included communications. There may be no greater example of this striving than in the period between 1967 and 1973 when Fred Turner decentralized the system during a massive expansion. Under decentralization, the regional offices—as opposed to the Oak Brook home office—supported the operators and company stores within each geographical area. For operators, this meant streamlining the communication cycle by providing immediate access to the local officers, the regional managers, who over time knew their territories more intimately than anyone else in management.

Decentralization, with its streamlined communications, sped up the decision making, as Rick McCoy, a one-time 90-store operator, mentioned to me. Prior to decentralization, owner/operators posed concerns directly to the main office in Oak Brook, skipping over the local regional office, basically jumping the chain of command. And that action would not always be met with an embrace. As Rick reminded me: "Fred, first thing would say to you is that he will get back to you. And then he would call the regional manager and ask two questions, 'What do the stores look like?' and 'How do they run?' And if they looked good and ran well, the conversation with Fred would continue, but if they didn't look good or ran poorly, that was the end of the conversation and you had to straighten it out with the regional manager first."

And as current executive vice president and chief restaurant officer, Jeff Stratton told me, "In the past it got too centralized. Centralized doesn't give you a good connection with what's really going on in the field. We now talk about what's going on all the time. We trust our leaders [in the field] to bring those issues to us, and we address them."

Under decentralization, however, regional managers decided on real estate acquisition and development, as well as licensing decisions, and many times utilized their own boards of operators to help facilitate resolutions. Boards consisting of marketing, public relations, and operations were developed to establish a process for information flow and getting critical input. This structure greatly aided in communication at all levels, and is a model of how an organization can grow and yet remain responsive to the local market's needs. Still, even with decentralization Fred Turner was mindful of keeping the lines of communications open. In a note to company partners, Fred wrote: ". . . We've got to chip away at our own bureaucracy. We've got to push harder than ever for the basic principles that made us what we are."

143

To this day, CEO Jim Skinner is a firm advocate of decentralization and keeping the decisions closest to the marketplace, be that a region in the United States or another country entirely. Again, this was really an extension of Ray and Fred's idea of seeking to get as much information and engaging those closest to the customer for ideas, and those who understood the culture and the local political process as well.

Decentralization was as critical then as it is today. "Communication from the regional manager is far more important than some executive VP or me, semiworking, semiretired, but trying to keep his hand in to help however I can," Fred told me.

Fred understood the importance of keeping the authority within the regions. Decentralization works well as long as the facts are communicated effectively and those in power respect that the final decision should be deferred to the field. The channels of communication should discourage people from bypassing regional management but keep the chain of command intact by allowing the regions the first dialogue and opportunity to have discussion, leaving conversations with the corporate office as the avenue of last resort.

Retired CEO Jack Greenberg put it this way: "In a franchising system, a highly decentralized business model which the business required, it wasn't a philosophical question . . . about centralized versus decentralized, because you can't do franchising in real estate or run retail operations without having a decentralized system. You have to get people understanding what you

Food for Thought

How can your organization's structure be molded to enhance communication?

Regionalization, or decentralization, can be an effective organizational structure, and can play a critical role in communications within an organization. Some thoughts:

- Pick individuals who have the skills, talents, and leadership to run independently.
- Allow these individuals the responsibility and the authority to make decisions.
- Establish a solid relationship of communication that allows those in the field and corporate headquarters to bounce ideas and issues off each other (so that the regions are independent, yet not alone).
- Whenever possible, have individuals that understand the local market.
- Use an "earn the right to be left alone" process. Simply put, this means that as an individual gains more experience and tenure in the specific area, greater authority can be relinquished by headquarters.

are asking them to do and wanting them to do it. And I think that is all about communications and salesmanship and trust."

Yet decentralization did not remove corporate staff from getting into the action. Instead, the key executives made it a point to visit the regions, presenting those of us in the regional offices with the distinct advantage of access to some of the top experts in the company. And we had open communication with these key experts. For accounting issues, we had ready access to Gerry Newman, McDonald's chief accounting officer, who always figured out a way to structure favorable financing for licensees. In real estate matters, we looked to Win Christiansen, former senior vice president for Worldwide Restaurant Development, who had tremendous experience working with developers. With market research we turned to Jim Rand, vice president, marketing, McDonald's who headed global expansion for McDonald's and intimately understood the potential sales volume for each new store and how that potential would affect existing stores. For advertising, Paul Schrage, retired senior executive vice president, was renowned for his ability to connect with consumers and to build a brand. For legal, Don Horowitz, retired McDonald's executive VP and chief legal counsel, comprehended the legal challenges operators faced in each of the regions and kept many of us out of trouble. And for franchising, we sought Burt Cohen, retired senior vice president of licensing, who had a deep understanding of the legal aspects pertaining to licensing and maintaining the integrity of the system. These individuals spent time working with the regions and providing support for these key areas, and they were some of the best in the industry in their particular areas. As Bob Weissmueller, former McDonald's vice president who became CEO of Fazoli's, commented on Gerry Newman making visits to the regions: "The time that Gerry would spend, coming out to the regions and really helping you understand the business, and how to work through your individual problems, really helped to develop your broader business sense. It made me a smarter businessperson. It didn't matter if it was construction or Paul Schrage in advertising helping at an operator meeting, you knew they were all about the same thing, and you learned so much."

Open Communications

Even the look and feel of the home office in Oak Brook says that McDonald's is a company that values the exchange of ideas. There was an open-door policy—literally no doors on offices— a feature that was ahead of its time in the 1970s, and, that with very few exceptions is still prevalent to this day. This environment encourages collaboration and communication between everyone. And it demonstrates the transparency both of the company and in the relationships between stakeholders.

It lends itself to the type of communications that can be so effective in informal meetings. In the book *Good to Great*, Jim Collins relates to the effective use of these meetings: "The good to great leaders made particularly good use of informal meetings where they'd meet with groups of managers and employees with no script, no agenda or set of action items to discuss." These informal sessions, called "town hall meetings" for large groups, can be particularly effective, as Collins notes.

That openness was evident in the company's earliest days, right on the restaurant floor. The openness of the original red-and-white unit design, dubbed a "fishbowl" because it allowed customers to observe the kitchen, communicated to the public that the kitchens were spotless at a time when the 15-cent hamburger was novel, driving many folks to question the quality of the product.

Later, as a regional manager, although I did add a conference room with a door, I embraced that openness in my own office with that open-door policy, which encouraged the staff to pop in for a chat if I wasn't already meeting with someone. That accessibility is still apparent today, as I discovered during a recent visit to Oak Brook when meeting with CEO Jim Skinner. By its very design, that openness communicates to staff that there are no secrets, and it encourages dialogue.

This spirit of open communications is favored today by forward-thinking leaders, including New York City mayor Michael R. Bloomberg, who transformed City Hall into an open-bullpen environment, with the mayor at its center, approachable and open to an exchange of new ideas.

Communicating the Brand

McDonald's is forever striking a chord with consumers. Its memorable slogans from its "you deserve a break today" ditty in 1971, to its "two all-beef patty" jingles in 1974, to its current global "I'm lovin' it" campaign keeps McDonald's one of the most recognized brands in the world.

But those efforts require careful communications with the company's creative team, as former chief marketing officer Paul Schrage told me: "Our whole thing was that a hamburger is a hamburger—but then there's a McDonald's hamburger. And what we tried to do was add dimension to that hamburger. Add additional meaning. It isn't just meat, bread, and potatoes. You get a lot more with a McDonald's hamburger, and we tried to create that with our advertising," Paul noted.

Open discussions and careful listening played an important role in the ultimate communication of the brand. "You wanted to make sure that the creatives [the creative people on the team] felt they always had a fair and just evaluation of their work— that their work would be looked at, listened to, considered," Paul continued. "Any idea is something for us to look at and consider. In no way would you do or say anything that would embarrass them. You wanted them to feel that, and rightly so, because we believed it. I believed it. We had to get the best from these folks,

147

and we wanted them to be thinking about us all the time. We recognized that they worked with other clients—that's life in the agency business—but we know by giving them the audience and giving them the open evaluation and when we would review creative, it was a matter of literally going around the room and getting comments from everybody. Then, of course, in the end it would come down [to] one person . . . eventually [having] to make that decision. And that's how they were judged."

As Paul pointed out to me, if a piece of work was not accepted, the creatives understood why. "There was no mystery," Paul said. "They knew exactly what we liked, what we disliked, and the changes that needed to be made." The process included further revisions, and open communications that fostered the back and forth that evolved into some of McDonald's best campaigns. "It was the openness that they always felt they had, and I knew from dealing with creatives over here that was something that they just didn't experience in a lot of other companies," Paul said.

And the branding didn't stop with the jazzy ad campaigns, as CEO Jim Skinner shared with me: "Everything that's internal is external. Everything is messaging. . . . Messaging about the brand on a physical basis, you drive onto our lot, you drive onto our brand."

The Importance of Back and Forth

In the uniqueness of the three-legged-stool system, communication was critical. But that back and forth meant more than just easy access to stakeholders. And it also meant more than listening. It also meant compromise. These traits, along with teamwork and collaboration were the hallmarks of the three-legged-stool principle. It was predicated on all three of its members having input; it forced collaboration, and its by-product was compromise. "There is input from all parties involved to try and make a collective good decision to help the brand," noted Jeff Stratton. "We are all at the table together. And it is the spirit of collaboration. And while at the end of the day, the company has to make the decision, they are respectful of that, but appreciate that they have had their say."

As Peter Grimm, a 35-year supplier of buns as well as owner of a distribution organization for the system, told me: "This is not a top-down deal, you can't stuff things down an independent businessman's throat, and the independent businessman can't make the franchisor do what he wants all of the time. This is a place where you have to understand compromise; this is not black and white all the time. There is a lot of gray, and to navigate and survive you need to understand what shades of gray there are and how to deal with them." That flow of give and take and understanding each other's position helped to train many of the management within the system.

It was also working with operators, who, by their very nature are strong, independent entities. (Didn't we want strong and successful people in our operator ranks?) So egos, personalities, and sheer intelligence were always at play as well.

These gatherings are still part of the culture, all the way up the corporate ladder. Jeff Stratton spoke with me about a tradition leading up to the company's food-improvement committee sessions. "One of the things that we did was we had a dinner with that group, and now we do this all over the world," he told me. "We have dinner with the group the night before the meeting, every single time; we never miss. And while the purpose of that dinner is social, one memorable time Fred told us about a number of stories, and it became emotional for him, but was very positive. Jim [Skinner] has done that with his experience with the management team as well."

Back when I was a restaurant manager, I realized people listened when you had something to express. Rick McCoy spoke about the importance of communications in the field: "It's a multi-billion-dollar organization, but you can pick up the phone and get a hold of someone, a callback. The operators know that they can go right up to the top people and have a conversation. They look you right in the eye; they don't look over your shoulder to see who's coming next."

Although I never doubted the importance of communications in business, I didn't fully appreciate it until serving on a management team in 1974 that ran individual restaurants for a New York franchisee. We held monthly meetings, reviewing operations, profits, and people on a regular basis. We'd go around the room and be put on the spot to respond and report on each area—and it forced us all to do our homework as well as hone our skills in speaking and communicating effectively.

One of my favorite perks of the job was the post-meeting dinners, eye-opening affairs for most of us in the 1960s, coming from lower-middle-class or blue-collar households and having never dined out that often. It was an entirely new experience, and besides making us appreciate a fine dining experience, it provided an outstanding forum for discussion, debate, and lively conversation. This, too, proved to be another opportunity to learn and absorb how to conduct business discussions—or, maybe sometimes, how not to! I learned to enjoy having my own disagreements and conversations with my peer group. It was both encouraged and expected. Just like the fry man in the restaurant, who was frowned upon for not keeping up with the rush of customers in the store, you had to join in the fray and participate, lest you be viewed as too quiet. Your opinions mattered. Though I didn't realize it at the time, we were developing the communication skills we'd need as we climbed the corporate ladder.

I enjoyed the lively conversations. I began forming my own opinions on subjects about business issues such as increasing sales, managing personnel issues, and more. And I did my best to keep up with the more senior members of the group. Our animated discussions, on more than one occasion, prompted the restaurateurs to warn us to either keep it down or leave. These spirited gatherings were, in fact, part of the culture, and often made for good stories, particularly the time we got booted out of the legendary Palm restaurant in Manhattan for being a bit too lively. Mixed in with that good-natured fun was the opportunity to express ourselves comfortably, building relationships and opening the door for future collaborations. The arguments that ensued hardly mattered—we were advancing our discussions in a manner that was centered around business but still fun. As Ed Rensi mentioned, "Debate intelligently."

Lesson Learned

It's important to keep communication light, lively, and fun at a group function. It's the leader's responsibility to ensure that

1. Everyone gets involved.
2. People don't step on each other in conversation, and everyone has his or her say.
3. The culture is nurtured in such a way that it becomes a given that everyone's opinion counts.
4. The conversation does not get into areas that can be uncomfortable or inappropriate.
5. The leader's role is to facilitate.

I tried to absorb all that transpired in these conversations, grasping the various styles of each participant. Ultimately, I decided that while volume and speed of conversation helped, in the end, it was style and content that really mattered. You had to know your facts and be able to back them up. This group was not giving up anything without solid backups of your position. Again, the ability to intelligently argue a differing opinion was a great start for a future career in corporate management and working with independent licensees. It wasn't about the brawn anymore, or position power, as it had been on the restaurant floor; it was about the preparation, knowledge of the facts, and style.

As my persuasion skills developed, my colleagues looked to me to make small presentations or lead discussions within the group at various meetings. Supported by my franchisee at the time, a powerful and dynamic speaker himself, I became more proficient. The ability to express my opinion, contrary or not, became an integral part of my personality.

Lesson Learned

It's important to question, but it is equally important to question in the right way. As Ed Acre, a McDonald's licensee, once pointed out to me: "It's okay to disagree, but don't be disagreeable." Taking Ed's words to heart, I also made it a point to always give an alternative solution, not just to disagree.

McDonald's manual of core competencies for staff touts the importance of giving "open and honest and timely communication." As Roland Jones commented in his book *Standing Up & Standing Out*: "I characterize the everyday flow of communication as organic rather than bureaucratic. Without a rigid hierarchy, good ideas bubble upward. An effective leader keeps his feet on the ground and his door open, with his lights on—thus being available for everyone on the team."

I asked Ed Rensi about his ideas of communicating and his methods to speak to such a large organization. He replied: "I found out early on, if you don't tell your story, the rumor mill will, the grapevine will. Or outside influences will. There was a period when McDonald's was in a lot of stress, and I sent a letter a month to all of our employees at their homes addressed to Mr. and Mrs. Whomever. I must have written dozens of letters over those months, and I addressed it to the family. I called them McFamily letters. It was about 'this is what we are doing, this is why we are doing it, this is what we want to achieve, and this is how the marketplace looks.' Because if the company doesn't tell its strategic story . . . who is going to?" The format also helped relay a message of unity, that we were all in this moment together, and that it too would pass.

One of the clear messages was the idea of "selling" versus telling in business conversations. Fred Turner mentioned to me that "communication is crucial, it's more sell than telling. A crucial part of communication is the visionary aspect, and in terms of future development, the visionary goes without saying . . . it's vital." And it's true—the leader must continuously reinforce the vision, the direction of where the group is going. Ray was the key to communications in the early formidable years. His skills as a salesperson were paramount in his ability to instill enthusiasm and interest in his fledging concept. As Fred mentioned, "Ray was more approachable than I was. He was a great conversationalist. He was interested in people, had a genuine interest in people—he was a salesman's salesman. He was a peddler in the best sense of the word. He loved to tell stories, jokes." Those jokes and stories got his audience to relax, enjoy their time with Ray, and in their ease, they listened to him, and as many have confessed, became believers in the system.

In talking with Willis Smart, a former McDonald's regional vice president, and now an operations vice president with Dunkin' Brands, he mentioned to me the importance of telling stories. "The storytelling that goes on because of the unbelievable history of the organization at McDonald's really does set the culture. If I'm starting today, I don't know if I could ever have the same emotional attachment to it that I developed over the 30 years I worked there," he said, adding that the rich storytelling that has become part of McDonald's folklore bridges the gap for those entering the system in the post–Ray and Fred years. Willis continued: "The moral of it was [that] when you tell stories, this stuff is real, this stuff really happened. The crazy things, all the way through to the fabulous opportunities."

The idea of storytelling and legacy building, handed down from generation to generation within an organization, is not unique. From the Sam Waltons in retail, to the Lee Iaccocas in auto manufacturing, to Walt Disney, Vince Lombardi, and Henry Ford in other industries, there are thousands of stories and legends that are passed by each successive management team within an organization. That folklore becomes part of the culture of the company. Most of the stories are based on some real-life incident, which in most cases happened many years earlier, and most have been somewhat misstated a bit by now, but they serve to pass on corporate values. But the stories that circulate often stem from employees, and sometimes these stories aren't always good—some can be downright cruel. That's one reason why many an executive has used the "grapevine" for the distribution of information, as a tool rather than as a defensive action. The method couldn't be simpler. Share a positive message in the group—and watch it spread. And you should, as any good marketer would, take advantage of the various mediums available, from podcasts to blogs, to spread a story.

Conventions, retreats, dinners, and other corporate gatherings are the perfect vehicles for storytelling, as well as legacy building. As Jeff Stratton told me: "In a lot of our communications you will get a lot of the heritage, a lot of our things like conventions, the managers speaking of their experiences that we are doing all over the globe. We never conduct one of those without talking about Ray and Fred. We never talk about significant communication pieces going out without talking about the focus on the core of our business and the roots of our business. We built a very strong foundation." Willis added further to Jeff's comments: "If you want to build a service culture in the organization, you have to do storytelling so that people understand what it is that gets rewarded."

And, as Jeff pointed out, the legacy building serves to foster relationships, even among people with whom you have never worked directly but who benefit from the work you do. "A lot of those people that were at the McVeteran's event helped us [build a foundation]," Jeff told me, referring to the McDonald's alumni organization that met at the April 2008 convention. He added this example: "I said something to one of our older veteran operators when I was there. He called me over; I didn't personally know him very well. I knew of his restaurants. He called me over just to say 'thank you,' for the momentum of the business and the focus, because he had been out of it and coming back and seeing that he was just blown away. I then said to him, and another veteran operator, something I have heard our executive team say before: 'We stand on the shoulders of those that have gone before us, and the fantastic foundation you have built for us, so I thank you. So it's very important to me that we preserve that legacy.'"

Lesson Learned

There are many creative ways to communicate, on all levels. Here is a partial list of some types of events and media that companies use and suggestions for effective ways to communicate with them; they can be adapted for almost any organization:

Newsletters: state-of-the-company presentations

Storytelling: an open-door environment

Retreats: advisory boards

Rap sessions: staff blogs

Podcasts: performance appraisals

Town hall meetings: quotations

Social activities: informal conversations

Dinners, lunches, breakfasts: use of humor

Letters; e-mail, and snail mail: video or CD messages

Ceremonies: nonverbal communication

Meetings with agendas: focus group sessions

"Windshield time": what we at McDonald's commonly referred to as one-on-one time in a car with an individual out in the field touring restaurants

Impact of Technology

In today's era of increased technology, are we really communicating better? With the advent of virtual offices, e-mail, personal digital assistants (PDAs), teleconferencing, and individuals working in home offices, it seems that traditional communications are at risk. Texting and e-mailing are on the rise, with 58 percent of adult Americans using cell phones or PDAs to do at least one of 10 mobile nonvoice data activities, according to research by the Pew Internet & American Life Project in 2008. I spoke with Ron Bailey, a six-store franchise who had his doubts as to the efficacy of online communications. "I think one of the mistakes, just using technology when you rely on e-mails, you e-mail a ton of stuff to us, and we didn't read it, there is just so much. I don't want my manager sitting on a computer all day," he said. In the earlier days, "we had retreats (with operators) and consultants spending more time in the restaurants." Those simple methods of communication seemed to resonate with many people with whom I spoke.

Still, technology is essential in a $64 billion global company, and becomes even more prevalent as the company continues to grow, as Jeff Stratton told me. "I personally am very supportive of it [e-mail]," Jeff said. But, I think those of us who have history with the company are also still into picking up the phone when we get the letter or picking up the phone when we get the comment, and dealing with it personally. I know I do, and I'm only speaking for myself. Fred still does when he gets input. I know Jim does, I have personally seen him do it."

And the back and forth doesn't have to stop with phone calls, as Mike Roberts, retired McDonald's former president, told me: "I think communications is the lifeblood of trust. I would try every week to write 25 handwritten notes to somebody—a restaurant manager, an operator who was having difficulties, or a company employee I was impressed with. It was another way to say you're appreciated. And nobody ever expected to get a handwritten letter or a phone call. But when you do get it, hey, the president of the company is on the phone and he wants to talk with you . . . [you've] got to be kidding. And it helped to galvanize the people." Roland Jones added to this point by noting: "You need to establish trust with the people you lead. A leader seeks opportunities to establish dialogue because *communication* establishes that nature of the relationship."

Lesson Learned

While e-mail plays an important role in relaying messages, don't allow it to substitute for the value of a conversation, whether in person or by phone. Communicating is often better conveyed in plain, old-fashioned conversations—the ultimate building block in any relationship. Communication occurs only when both participants receive and understand the information. Sending an e-mail is not a replacement for conversation.

Still, there is no question that in a growing organization, internal communication is often not ideal—a challenge McDonald's navigates this way: "We do our best to make sure that what we want to convey, everybody hears it," Bob Marshall, the vice president of U.S. restaurant operations, said to me. "Everybody that comes in here hears the exact same thing. So I think we pay particular attention in making sure the message is singular, and no matter where you sit you are going to be hearing the same thing."

Jeff Kindler, currently the CEO of Pfizer and a former McDonald's executive, told me his thoughts on communicating and the experiences he took away from his McDonald's tenure. He still adheres to the time-tested methods of communicating to his staff.

"When McDonald's acquired Boston Market, the company also gained 30,000 employees who had worked for a bankrupt company, had gone through five CEO's in a short time, and were disillusioned. And as the new leader of this group, I faced the challenge of creating energy and optimism that the business needed to succeed. So I traveled all over the country during the first six months of that job, doing town hall meetings, giving straightforward answers to any and all questions, and helping people feel good about what they were doing. This experience taught me leadership lessons that apply to any business, and I still use them today. With a company of Pfizer's size, there's no one-size-fits-all approach to building a sense of community and creating a shared vision throughout all our global locations. To achieve this, I try to talk face to face with as many people as possible. I travel a lot, and we have some pretty frank discussions about our future together. I believe it's just as important to acknowledge the reality of our challenges as it is to be optimistic about the potential of our opportunities. Open communications play a big part at any company in creating the right culture to succeed."

159

The Power of Good Information

Later in my career, as I became a director of operations for the corporation, I learned the importance of communication in a number of ways. In that position, I was second-in-command to the regional vice president, and that role proved to be a real learning experience in the realm of communications, as many times I saw the need to interpret the "what and why" to confused franchisees—and they looked to me for interpretation.

I devoted a lot of time with staff and operators, explaining what we were doing, as they would tend to try and get me to come in between them on an issue with the regional manager. It required that I was knowledgeable about everything that went on, making effective communication mandatory. Still, it allowed me to get inside all decisions as they were made and watch how the process—and sometimes the lack of process—led to actions. It forced me to explain the regional manager's perspective with an objective factual side, which showed me that good decisions are made with a balance of both.

On one notable episode, the regional manager literally left the restaurant in disgust over steeper-than-suggested menu board pricing, not wanting to get into an argument with the operator. Suddenly, I was left there trying to resolve the situation with the operator. I managed to get the conversation back on track and even convinced the operator to compromise after some careful review. By this point, after all the lively debates with my colleagues, I was well versed in expressing solid points even in the most heated scenarios. So, I reached into my repertoire of tools to communicate to the operator the importance behind the pricing and to say that I'd smooth things over with the regional manager.

It also forced me into a deep understanding of the power of good information and how it can sway the decision-making process. All too often I had witnessed "decision paralysis" that many otherwise talented individuals could not get past—they simply lacked the ability to make a decision and consider its impact on leading a group of people. In many cases that inability to react and make decisions prevented some from achieving their potential, or simply becoming more effective leaders.

Lesson Learned

All decisions should be made with three key essentials:

1. Factual data and research
2. Input from staff and individuals close to the situation
3. Your own instincts and experience

Displays

While verbal and written communications are the stuff of everyday life, some messaging deserves to be expressed in an altogether different format. Just as Jim Skinner displays the Plan to Win strategy on the wall, mission statements, quotes, and portraits are other examples of effective methods for conveying a company's values and heritage. As I spoke by phone with Jeff Stratton, he said, "The wall I'm looking at, there is a picture of Fred on the left, on the right is a picture of Ray, and right in the middle is Jim Cantalupo. So that legacy is there." And Don Horowitz reminded me of an unusual display, a piece of glass which is about half an inch thick and measures approximately 24-inches-by-6-feet that is etched

One on One with Jim Skinner

In my pursuit to better understand the role communications continues to play at McDonald's, I had lunch in an Oak Brook conference room with CEO Jim Skinner (a Big Mac for me, a salad for Jim). In continuing McDonald's upward tick, Jim places great importance on the company's Plan to Win strategy, which is clearly communication of a direction and goal. The Plan to Win features the 5 P's: People, Products, Place, Price, and Promotion. He is diligent about updating the document, mentioning that it is pretty timeless in nature. To keep the plan not only alive but also relevant, it touches all levels of the system, right down to the store managers and crew—there's nothing lofty or ivory-towered about it. And to showcase its importance, Plan to Win—which, in its earliest phase was a true collaboration effort by the top McDonald's executives at the time: Jim Cantalupo, Charlie Bell, and Jim Skinner. As he furthers the initiative to drive the company forward in today's challenging times, Jim displays the Plan to Win on the wall just outside his office.

with an ever-evolving timeline featuring all the past and present board members in the history of McDonald's. It is mounted on the wall outside the boardroom at the campus office. "In the early years, Fred said, 'I want to see something different. I want to see something that no one has ever done before,'" Don said. "And you look at that plaque, which shows the history of the company in the form of the board of directors, and you see something that you would not see at any other corporate headquarters, which is interesting. It is something that grows, and was designed so that it is never obsolete, it's always changing." This artwork communicates the heritage and culture of the organization.

The Pitch

Licensing new restaurants to operators has been without doubt one of the toughest kinds of decisions a regional manager makes, one that dramatically impacts a franchisee's profits. Not taking these decisions lightly, we based decisions on three essentials: factual data and research, input from staff and other stakeholders, and our own experience and gut instincts. In order to more fully allow for good communications on these serious decisions, we developed a process, called a "pitch," for getting all the pertinent information on the table prior to a decision. Operators were invited to pitch their case; we provided them an opportunity to express to us the rationale as to why they were best suited for growth. These were great sessions, with many of us gaining great insights to what was happening in the field and what was on the operators' minds. Some became real "dog-and-pony" shows, so we had to balance the style and presentation with the facts. This process forced them to deeply examine the various aspects of their operation with the factual data that we both shared. It gave greater credence to the importance of our reviews of their operations and reaffirmed the five criteria that we established in order for them to be considered expandable.

Then as a team, my staff and I evaluated the pros and cons behind the decision. In almost every case, we all came to the same conclusion. All of us internally at least, could justify the decision and how we got there, which included giving the operators the opportunity to express the strengths of their organization. And there was another very valuable added aspect. Because the individuals in the field, closest to the operators who might question the wisdom of a decision, were part of the process, it gave them the rationale, the "why," to explain intelligently the transaction. All too often, those in the field, closest to the action, are seldom given the reasoning behind a decision.

This kind of process has application in a number of different organizations in a variety of scenarios. For example, an organization looking to fill a position can ask candidates for their pitch, as can an organization interviewing new vendors and suppliers. Allow them to "strut their stuff," and you gain another opportunity to learn more before arriving at a decision.

163

Responding to a Need

The best resolutions are often derived from talking things through with your team. Back in 1992, as regional vice president of McDonald's, I chaired the meeting of department heads with my group, and we grappled with the realization that we were not going to meet our profit plan—an often recurring struggle that is familiar to many corporate officers and businesspeople within their business lives. In our usual fashion, we reviewed the usual key metrics that were our goals for the year. And when we all realized our dilemma, we took the time for each of the department heads to review how that person might contribute from his or her respective department. All of the disciplines represented were not directly linked to solving an immediate profit crisis . . . and yet, each contributed in his or her own way. In a surprise to all of us, we discovered our solution from one of the least likely areas: real estate. Our real estate team, under director of development Ernie Annibale, had been working on the possibility of selling air rights to developers within the specific areas of some of our locations in Manhattan. These were quite valuable to the developers, as it allowed them to "buy" the rights to develop a larger and taller building within our market. A block was regulated as to how much "mass" could be developed in a particular parcel. We found the solution to our immediate problem by working collaboratively and communicating with our leadership team. And that also led the way for additional deals from properties owned throughout the region, which over the years returned millions of dollars in previously unfound revenue to both the company and the operators whose stores were involved and who subsequently received, in many cases, a proportionate share of the monies for remodeling or upgrading in the process.

164

"Hotter, Faster"

I was reminded of a unique example of communicating an important issue by Willis Smart, who recalled a time when McDonald's focus was redirected toward a back-to-basics agenda. Ed Rensi, then the president of the company, solved it in his own way. "It was symbolic," said Willis. "Ed wrote a book, called *Hotter, Faster*, and the entire book had only those two words. It was very grounded in the importance of operations and that we were an operations-driven company." Ed knew the value of finding a new way to communicate important messaging, and as crazy as the format was, it sure got our attention.

The Ability to Challenge

One of the more interesting anomalies within the scope of communicating in the McDonald's system has been the pervasive encouragement to challenge and to question. In a seemingly straight-laced, formulized structure, outsiders looking into the organization are always amazed at the allowance and encouragement of creativity. It's been said by many, that McDonald's is really a "tight-loose" type of organizational structure in many ways, a structure that again owes itself to Ray Kroc, Fred Turner, and others. Don Horowitz had this to say about this phenomenon: "Ray was a guy who always listened to a new idea and to . . . how you could do something better, and God knows, we thought we had a good formula, and we were doing things right." Still, through communications, Ray went all out to make the system even better.

And this style was not lost on Fred Turner who, in turn, adopted many of Ray's qualities of leadership himself. "Fred encouraged people to try new things," said Don. "Fred's question always was, 'How are we going to do it differently—how are you going to include this and do it better?' And early on that [Fred's asking this question] meant that many times you were not taking enough risks. Well, if someone says that to you, that gives you a certain amount of freedom in terms of taking some risk." Risk taking was permeated in the culture, and we were constantly encouraged to articulate our ideas as a way to think plans through so that the best ideas had a real shot at becoming a success.

No ideas or programs went without challenge. Such deliberations made the process arduous, to be sure, but it also made the company stronger. Think of Paul Schrage's view.

In his role as McDonald's chief marketing executive, he was directly responsible for the advertising and marketing of the organization. But, in order to advertise on national media, he *needed the approval* of the operator organization, called OPNAD (Operators National Advertising fund), to spend those funds. That meant investing a huge amount of effort to "sell" to the operator community the business logic for a particular campaign. And just to make it more difficult, every store in every region did not necessarily share the same response . . . so many operators had difficulty understanding the logic behind whatever you were proposing and how it related to them locally. This led to some pretty intense discussions between the corporation and the licensees. But many times this process also had a tendency to help a campaign develop and morph into a better one with their input. It was all about synergy and respect for one another's position. As Paul saw it, "As we grew, it became obvious that you couldn't do that [make decisions out of one central location]. And at about that point in time, I truly started to appreciate the worth of all the exchange we had, and how difficult it was, if you presented your case to the operators, and you got some good discussion, . . . to get [a] good [resolution] out of it. I don't believe that we [were ever denied] our approval when we presented [our case] well to the operators. And I believe to this day, I believe all the grinding, bumping, and side-door meetings, all the stuff that would go on, like a political process, gave us the best product, and that's the product we have today, and we continue to achieve it by going through the process. It did lead us." At McDonald's, the tougher the process, the better the result—the weaker ideas, while vetted, never stood a chance.

Many times the operators went along with decisions solely for the good of the system. As retired CEO and chairman Mike Quinlan noted, "Many have enough faith in the McFamily that they are willing to subjugate their personal preferences enough for the greater good of the whole, so they go along with it."

Good organizations seek to improve communications by examining even the most mundane or insignificant activities. Consider, for example, performance appraisals or reviews that are conducted, usually annually, on employees within an organization. Without expanding on the merits, or perhaps the downside of these activities, few would quibble with the notion that if employees do not understand what is expected of them, and do not have the tools to accomplish the tasks they are assigned, the chances of success are minimal. And its importance is huge.

Performance Appraisals

In an article for *HR Magazine* in August 2005, Kathryn Tyler states: "The performance appraisal is the most powerful and misused tool for improving the performance of employees." Performance appraisal systems were prevalent throughout McDonald's in one form or another over the years. Being on both sides of that equation, I can fully understand the value or, in some cases, the downside or perception of these reviews. The point is, whether it was an employee, an operator, or even a vendor (in the case of an annual review of their organization), it is a wonderful opportunity to have open, honest dialogue. This avenue of communication is a great occasion not only to improve communications but also to review how well performance goals are being met. The employee who is totally shocked and surprised by his or her review, or the operator who hears comments for the first time, clearly indicates that there is a void in clear communications. People are not communicating their expectations, observations, or thoughts effectively. When that's the case, how can we expect improvement? We need to be communicating performance issues all the time. Perhaps Tom Peters, in his book *Thriving on Chaos*, says it best: "A person who is genuinely and legitimately surprised by his or her annual performance appraisal provides grounds for dismissal of the person's boss." While that may be extreme, the point is made: *Good communications should be indicative of a no-surprises process. If that is not the case, one needs to dig deeper.* All of us should take the time to evaluate how well we really are communicating with our staff.

Jack Welch, in his book *Straight from the Gut*, states, "If I learned anything about making this easier [about removing people], it's seeing to it that no one should ever be surprised when they are asked to leave. By the time I met with managers I was about to replace, I would have had at least two or three conversations to express my disappointment and to give them the chance to turn things around."

167

In interviewing numerous individuals for this book, I was amazed and surprised at the amount of conversation that the issue of "talking to each other" came up in discussion, even though years had passed with many of their careers. In some cases, it was painfully clear that there were unresolved feelings. I believe much of these feelings could have been avoided with more frank, honest communication at all levels and at numerous times.

Food for Thought

How can organizations make performance reviews more effective?

Performance appraisals and other similar processes are a great opportunity to communicate and encourage engagement.

Unfortunately, many of the organizations I have worked with in my consulting practice seem to miss out on this kind of opportunity. Instead, they find performance reviews an arduous task—an unpleasant exchange for both the supervisor and the employee. How can you turn a performance appraisal into a more rewarding experience?

- Ask employees to come to the meeting prepared with their notes of appraisal comments from the previous review, as well as a list of accomplishments or activities that they felt good about during the previous review period.
- Deliver your review verbally, referring to notes, if necessary. However, don't just pull out a completed

written review, or employees will focus only on what is written on paper, rather than the importance of your dialogue. Also, by engaging in conversation, it demonstrates your willingness to hear their point of view, and that the final appraisal is not etched in stone yet—at least not until you've talked things through. This can only enhance the give and take.

- Keep the dialogue light and upbeat, focusing on key strengths and accomplishments.
- Listen to their feedback, concerns, and comments. You may be surprised—perhaps even change your mind about a performance—once you gather the facts from their perspective. I was surprised on more than one occasion by what I didn't know about an employee's achievements.
- Employees should not be surprised by the content of your review. If that element of surprise does exist, then you need to examine your communication during the year to understand why your message didn't come across sooner.
- Ask how you can help to make the job better, what training or additional support your employees could use, and how they perceive themselves within the organization.
- Look for the "button," the key to the employee that may come up during the conversation. It may be a hobby, an interest, a passion, or position aspired to. That may help to direct and engage them to a greater degree.

Protecting Reputation

Ed Rensi was right about telling your own story before the rumor mill spins out of control. I learned this firsthand as the regional vice president in New York in 1996 in the infamous rat-tail incident—as bizarre and unbelievable as this story may sound.

A customer allegedly purchased for his young son a Happy Meal and in it, the man claimed, was a fried rat's tail. The media ran with this story, airing it nonstop on television, radio, and newspapers. It was everywhere!

The operator, a good licensee, was aghast at all the hype and unwanted attention, and of course, sales immediately started to slow at that location. We went on immediate media action, taking a proactive approach and repudiating his claim that this could have happened in the restaurant. Citing our quality-control processes, we declared the rat-tail story impossible. Still, in these situations, the public decides you are guilty until proven otherwise—and the wisecracks from the media and late-night talk show hosts did not help at all.

But McDonald's, back in the early years, carried the scars of a similar experience years earlier, involving allegations that worms were in the hamburgers. It proved to be a hoax, of course, and initially did get some press, and Ray, in his own style, made light of it, passing it off as humorous that anyone in his or her right mind could believe it. It's not likely in today's media-savvy environment that such a pass would be given, and my experience certainly validated that.

On Long Island, this particular customer phoned the regional office, demanding money for damages. We immediately alerted the authorities, and they were very efficient in digging out the facts. We discovered that the tail was not your everyday rat's tail, but rather, one that is specific to lab rats used in experiments. Also, the tail in the incident was not fried in our vats, as the oil was different than ours. The crime was obvious.

Lesson Learned

Put a communications plan in place in order to prevent a story from spinning out of control. In the event of an unforeseen crisis or emergency, staff members should already know whom to call and which procedures to follow. Include in your plan the name of the company spokesperson who is skilled at handling the media, and ensure that that person is the only media contact. Make sure the staff understands the crisis plan.

In the end, a New Jersey doctor was convicted of mail fraud, wire fraud, and extortion for the scheme. Although the outcome was minimally reported by the media, it felt good that someone got nailed for trying to stick it to us. The good guys won that one.

171

In the Big Leagues

Proving myself as a decent communicator while serving as a director of operations, my regional manager at the time decided that I would be given the task of putting together the annual budget for the region. In the early years, it was an enormous undertaking that required weeks of preparation by the regional department heads before it was ready for review and a final edit. Every line item was scrutinized and justified by our group before it would be accepted in the final version. Once again, we all learned the importance of the details and how the sum total of many small budget amounts ultimately can have a large impact on the overall plan. When completed, we assembled it in a thick binder to present to top management in Oak Brook, after reviewing it with the zone office in Connecticut.

Budget preparation meant debating and challenging our team to justify the rationale behind each expense. It was also an opportunity to conduct a "people review" of the entire staff in order to predict raises and promotions. It was one of the few times we conducted our meetings behind the closed doors of our conference room. We used a board to list all of the staff and their respective positions. The personnel review was a powerful component of the process. We would chart out all of our individuals by department and discuss each one. The respective department head outlined each individual: his or her current position, where that person was going, the individual's potential to grow and skills needed. With the entire leadership team in the room, the dialogue was open and candid. It allowed everyone, regardless of area of expertise, to understand the importance of each staff member. Everyone gave input as we went around the room. It was often very interesting to hear others' perspectives as you gauge others' response to a person's opinion. Many times it validated how we saw our people; other times it did just the opposite. It was a blunt reminder of our main goal as department heads: to develop our people. The direction was clear. It is a process that all organizations should look to incorporate.

Finally, the day of scheduled budget review would arrive when it was time to present to a room filled with all the big guns: the president, chairman of the board, and top officers of each discipline. It was no laughing matter—not to mention a full-day affair where the dynamics were such that sometimes egos interfered as those at the top level jockeyed for position.

My team presented with our zone, which consisted of about six regions, with our senior vice president zone manager leading the way. While waiting for our region's scheduled time to present, we sat back and watched our peer group go through the wringer. We listened for buzzwords and topics, hoping to better understand which areas were most important to the top executives. We learned while we observed, tweaking our presentation as we noted which region's presentations were effective, and which were not.

Sometimes the battles bordered on the ridiculous. One year, an executive took exception to a region that had two of the same publications going to one office. It was a waste, he said, arguing that by having one subscription and sharing around the office, the region could save money. This dialogue went on for 20 minutes, all over a $15 subscription. Considering the number of issues that challenged the regional budgets, it seemed time could have been better spent. It was an example of how silly even our leadership team could be at times. I stored that one, hoping to keep it as a reminder of how frustrating stubbornness could be in a situation.

Still it was a lesson in being prepared to support and defend—or learn to compromise. In what amounted to great forums for debate, huge arguments sometimes ensued both within the executive ranks as well as with the region's defending themselves to the group. Everyone was exposed, and we saw again that it was okay to challenge, even though these discussions were often heated. At times, it was like a scene from the gladiators, as each side tried to gorge the other with its stated positions on a topic. We also gained insight as to what our neighboring regions were doing well and what could be shamelessly stolen. Actually, it was a fun process, but required that I knew everything that could possibly be thrown at me.

As the budget process fell on my lap of responsibility, I had to know that entire book. This meant doing my homework, and it drove me to learn aspects of the budget and line items that I normally would not have. I did not want to be embarrassed. I needed to know my facts and articulate those well—essentials in communicating effectively.

As difficult and painful as this process was, I believe it allowed the participants a rare opportunity and access to all of the company's top management. And, it presented a unique opportunity for many of us within the regions to showcase before this distinguished group. It worked well for everyone to get to know each other.

After hours of fighting over each line item, and reluctantly on occasion giving up on a budget item that we felt we really needed to run our region, Fred, and in later years Mike Quinlan, sometimes asked a simple question: "If you had the opportunity, forgetting the budget for a minute, what would you like to do in your region that would have impact?"

The question left us stunned. We were mentally beat up by the process, ready to slink out, feeling cut to the bone. The opportunity to make a positive impact on the region, by this point, was about the last thing on our mind. We were spent, literally and figuratively. Still, that the chairman asked our opinion indicated that he really cared about your opinion. So, with whatever fight we had left, we expressed how we really felt about an issue and more often than not the request *was granted*—giving us a boost after a really tough day. Even after being raked over the coals, we left the session with a win and the knowledge that we'd be able to return to our region with the ability to make a difference. We left feeling that the process wasn't so bad after all. And although we never realized it at the time, nor do I think management really understood it either, it was a very powerful learning experience in communications for everyone.

Lesson Learned

All organizations from time to time must tighten the belt by cutting to the extreme. But they also need a process to ensure that these cuts don't cause irreparable damage. In this process it is important to express a certain amount of flexibility. Otherwise, field experts who understand the nuances of the market will feel beat up in a budget process, stripped of their ability to do the right thing. And that can be very demoralizing.

In Summary

McDonald's has used communications to tell its story to the public. That story has helped build a culture that expresses its values to stakeholders, ultimately winning over customers and, as a result, shareholders. McDonald's has also looked to communications as an effective tool in helping it become a global leader. Through decentralization, McDonald's streamlined communications so that regional managers who knew their territories intimately were given the authority to render decisions expediently. By cultivating an environment where heated debates are welcome, the company developed a system of checks and balances, where only the very best ideas come forward. And because this environment is one where top leaderships expect answers when they asked, it forced us to stay on top of operations and really know our numbers. Organizations that demand as much in its approach to communications can push their way to excellence.

175

Key Learnings

✔ Communicate your company's goals, objectives, mission, and values. Continue the frequency of the message for commitment and understanding.

✔ Structure your company to encourage direct communications between stakeholders and the appropriate decision makers. Speak plainly.

✔ Design your place of business to foster a sense of openness throughout the company. Address any rumors or comments upfront and as quickly as possible.

✔ Remember that communications means not only the back and forth of ideas but also compromise. Ask for feedback. Encourage employee participation in as much decision making as possible.

✔ Promote communications between colleagues through lively, informative dinners and other gatherings that encourage open and honest debate.

✔ Challenge and question ideas respectfully, without getting personal. Learn intuitive listening, the ability to read the unspoken.

7

Recognition

I like to get people fired up, fill them with zeal for McDonald's, and watch their results in their work.

—Ray Kroc, *Grinding It Out: The Making of McDonald's*

As Ray Kroc knew, there is no better way to inspire a team than with recognition. Deep down, we crave that recognition. And the McDonald's culture is built on the foundation of rewarding hard workers. To outsiders, this probably doesn't sound like anything extraordinary—reward those who work hard, what's so groundbreaking about that? But at McDonald's, recognition was everywhere, at all levels, all the time. The culture is steeped in recognition, and as a consultant today I've yet to find a company that embraces recognition to that extreme. In my research, I discovered that on a national level McDonald's has tracked 23 different specific awards given to individuals—employees, suppliers, and licensees—and the years in which they were received. But these records tell only part of the story, as they do not take into account the zone and regional awards as well as worldwide recognition programs to those who, in the words of Ray Kroc, were filled with zeal for McDonald's.

The awards, regardless of the amount given out, were distinct from others given in most organizations I have worked with in two ways. First, these awards amounted to so much more than a plaque or a trip. Instead, they were given in sincere, heartfelt appreciation. As former regional vice president Willis Smart said to me, "The difference between us [McDonald's] and other organizations is that we are really genuine about what we are trying to do." Second, the celebratory aspect of the award—from the most humble pin or handshake to the highest possible honor bestowed on an employee—meant that there would always be an audience, be it family members or peers, to help in the commemoration. As McDonald's USA president Don Thompson put it, "We recognize people with fanfare." Added Willis, of his experience at winning the prestigious President's Award, "I couldn't get over the three-day celebration they had for us."

And David Delgado, formerly a real estate attorney at McDonald's and now a circuit court judge, reminded me how the company rewarded those who pushed forth with its mission to embrace diversity: "I was given recognition for joining a national Hispanic organization. Ed Schmitt, then the president of the company, came down to our area and congratulated me in front of the whole floor. The whole floor stopped what they were doing. I received a week at the corporate retreat in Lake Geneva. It encouraged other people to join organizations as well. It was impressive, and especially that they made such a big deal about it. He was very encouraging and supportive."

Ask anyone who ever rose within the ranks of the McDonald's system—from crew to operator to corporate—and he or she will tell you: We worked hard. And the recognition many of us received was satisfying in ways we never imagined possible.

Without that hard work, without the perseverance to sweat it out—whether serving as a counter person navigating the hectic lunch rush or as an officer in the Oak Brook home office growing the company globally—McDonald's arguably would never have attained such legendary success.

As a 16-year-old working my first McDonald's crew job, I drove myself hard to become part of the rhythm where everyone did his part (in the beginning, only males worked crew). Little did I know I was part of a system where those who delivered their consistent best were rewarded. Up until that point I hadn't realized the power of praise. But it got me. A little praise, some recognition, and I was ready to give my all to the company.

Now, it's easy to attribute that sort of revelation to youthful inexperience. Yet, the seasoned operators and executives I came to know who were also bestowed with all kinds of rewards, from winning incentive trips to opening additional stores to receiving a simple certificate, all share the same reaction. Consistently, they describe that reaction with these three words: "I was hooked." To this day, they still express the same kind of awe. All of us were achievers, answering to our own inner drive to excel, and subsequently were wowed when the system rewarded us. The system caught us by surprise.

179

As the American psychologist Abraham Maslow stated in *A Theory of Motivation*, people thrive on recognition as a form of self-value when they feel that their contributions make a difference. As humans, we need that affirmation. That's obvious. Yet even though recognition is such an affordable tool—it costs nothing to thank an employee for a job well done—you'd think more organizations would use it to engage their employees.

At McDonald's, recognition took many forms. There were promotions and raises, of course, but also weekends at one of the corporate ski lodges or condos, which were available to staff, not just to officers. And there were free dinners at wonderful restaurants. It didn't matter that many of us could foot the bill at a five-star restaurant ourselves; we were still dazzled by the thought of a night out on the company. But as retired senior executive Paul Schrage told me, "It recognized you as more than just that guy who comes to work every day."

And the use of recognition has other benefits as well. In an article entitled "Being Smart Only Takes You So Far" published in the January 2007 issue of *Training and Development*, the author, Bob Wall mentions: "Leaders should increase the amount of praise they offer to staff. Yet a recent Gallop Poll revealed that 65 percent of Americans haven't received recognition in the past year. A United States Department of Labor study found that the number one reason why people leave organizations is that they don't feel appreciated. The Gallup study found that increasing employee recognition lowers turnover, raises customer loyalty, and increases productivity."

Roots and Wings

McDonald's arguably takes employee recognition a step further than most organizations. Its home office includes "Partners Park," situated on McDonald's landscaped campus. The park features a circular wall on which is inscribed the names of every employee who has served the company for 25 years—a corporate version of a star on Hollywood Boulevard. The wall surrounds a huge bronze sculpture, a replica of the award that all partners receive to commemorate their 25 years at the firm. The sculpture is called "Roots and Wings," the phrase I've heard spoken by Fred Turner, the former chairman and CEO of McDonald's, now the company's honorary chairman. "Roots" is McDonald's very foundation—its standards, ethics, quality, service, and cleanliness (QSC). "Wings" evokes the latitude employees are given to tweak and prod the system in striving forward. Its message is clear.

The #1 Club

Roots and Wings is a concept that sets McDonald's apart from other franchises, in that it held us to the company's standards yet encouraged us to develop new and innovative ideas to improve the organization. Capturing this spirit and wrapping it around McDonald's penchant for recognition, I came up with an idea to develop our management trainee ranks back when I was a director of operations for a franchisee.

Understanding that our best success rate with talent was from development within, I wanted to continue that flow of individuals. Many of our crew viewed the job as a stopgap between schooling or getting into another career. These people, I knew, might be interested in continuing up the advancement ladder if they had a taste of it. So we formed the #1 Club, a chosen group consisting of the more senior and top-performing crew. They received a distinctive patch for their uniform, a raise, and the recognition of their peer group. To even be considered for this elite group was looked at as an honor by their peers. And they had to undergo a rigorous interview process as part of the review. Their main responsibilities included helping managers on the floor when needed and assisting in the many tasks of running the store.

Members of the #1 Club organized many of the crew's social functions and served as a sounding board for management to glean insights into the crew's perspective. It proved to be a great asset and was looked at by the corporation as a possible national program. Ultimately, the corporation established the "Crew Chief" position, which was somewhat of a similar idea for developing new talent.

Two of these #1 Club members actually went on to become owner/operators with their own organizations. One became a very successful midmanagement-level employee within the company. And one, Willis Smart, became a regional vice president for the corporation. Some 30-plus years later, Willis still recalls

181

the #1 Club vividly. "Do you know I still have my shirt with my patches?" he asked me recently. "Once I decided as a crew person that I think I wanted to do this, the next step was to make the #1 Club. You got performance reviews every month as a crew member back then, and you had to be rated outstanding for a full three months to even be considered, and then, any manager could veto your entrance into it. I think it was the thrill of recognition. I can remember it like it was yesterday." In the early days of the #1 Club, I, of course, had no idea it would leave such a lasting impression on its members. For some of our top performers, it turned out to be a more powerful motivator than I could have imagined.

From Shrines to Handshakes

Recognition has lingering aftereffects. I still have a wall adorned with my awards from McDonald's. These I show off with pride when visitors to my office inquire about them. And I'm not alone. Frank Behan, a former zone manager and senior vice president, refers to his stockpile of McDonald's awards as "a shrine." And retired senior executive vice president Paul Schrage, has a huge 4 × 5 painting of a Big Mac, which has sat prominently in the foyer of his house for the past 30 years. And around the corner is a display case of his 35-year career with the organization for all to see. And consider the sentiment of former McDonald's division president Debra Koenig, who, back in 1979, working in Philadelphia, won the President's Award, one of the company's most prestigious awards, given annually to the top one percent of all corporate employees.

"I won the President's Award only a few years into my time with McDonald's—and I was hooked," says Debra, who after 25 years at McDonald's served a stint as CEO at Vicorp, a chain of 250 family restaurants, headquartered in Denver, Colorado.

Even years later, Debra still remembers the President's Award, whose prize included a trip to Chicago for her and her husband, along with other high achievers in the company and their significant others. Debra won the award without even knowing it existed, attaining it because she was genuinely committed to contributing toward the McDonald's brand—in her case helping the corporation and franchisees drive down energy costs during the Jimmy Carter administration. Other awards and promotions followed, keeping her focused always on excellence. As Debra put it: "It motivated me to shoot for every other consequential award." Instinctively, Debra knew that "with a little effort" she would continue to earn the company's recognition. And while she appreciated the trips, new titles, and higher earnings, it was that recognition that seemed to her the most profound—and her thoughts parallel mine nearly exactly when I think about my own experience winning the President's Award. Said Debra: "McDonald's has made more folks than I can possibly imagine millionaires, and yet those millionaires get teary-eyed and turned on when they are given a plaque—the handshake is the most prestigious." Frank Behan made a comment about a letter he received upon retirement after 40 years of service to the company. "I got a lot of letters, but the one that hit home for me was the one from Fred that said, 'You made a difference.'" While those were only four words, the power of them, written by someone who really meant it, are tremendously influential.

183

Lesson Learned

A handshake is no doubt the least expensive way to recognize top performers—and perhaps the most effective. But simply remembering people's names is a great motivator as well, and equally cost effective. Make people feel important.

I hear similar sentiments from other McDonald's alumni, whether its former corporate people, vendors, or licensees. Visit their offices, and they are eager to reflect their best achievements and the high points in their careers. This is part of the McDonald's culture.

Ed Rensi told me: "I have boxes of plaques and photographs. . . . I don't want to get rid of any of this stuff because it means something to me. And when I do open it up, I go down memory lane in such an intense way that it's like . . . this is my memoir."

Building such a culture did not cost a whole lot of money—crystal paperweights, plaques, and letters of written praise do not require a huge cash outlay, but they sure pay back tenfold in creating lasting pride and motivation. Pat Paterno, who worked as a salesperson for a milk supplier beginning in 1958, spoke with me about the immense pleasure and pride he took when he was given a McDonald's ring, signifying 10 years of service for an employee or licensee. These were given out by the corporation on an annual basis. While receiving it was unusual in itself, as suppliers normally were not a direct part of the anniversary awards program, what made it even more poignant was the fact that the *operators* within the area he serviced bought it for him. Think about that: A group of customers so thankful to their vendor that they go out of their way to recognize him in a very personal way.

Team Awards

Awards that praise individuals are powerful tools, but team awards also can be equally effective and feature the added bonus of enabling a collaborative group celebrating the philosophy of Ray Kroc, who believed that "none of us is as good as all of us."

Back in 1971, for instance, I served as the manager of a new Long Island store when I was just 21 years old. We had our challenges, the biggest among them being that the area was just beginning a phase of major development, and though the population was expected to grow by leaps and bounds, it hadn't yet. That meant slow sales. So, as a team, we switched our priorities from growing sales to being the best possible in our operations.

Yet, toward the end of that first year, we received the recognition for which we all worked so hard—the A rating for the store. It was given by the corporation to those stores within the region that exemplified the very best in operational excellence and customer satisfaction. Everyone felt great and was proud of what we had accomplished.

A beautiful plaque was prominently positioned on the wall near our front counter, for all to view. Once again, the power of recognition was clearly and indelibly burned into my management toolbox. As Bob Weissmueller, a retired division vice president, recalled, recognition that was given out "spurred you on." He fondly recalled getting a magnum of champagne delivered to his office when he first became an officer. And the staff also received recognition for growing sales in those early years, as he recalled, in the form of a dozen roses delivered to the regional office from Ed Schmitt, then president of the company. As simple as that gesture was, everyone celebrated their achievement for that month.

Recognition for hard work was also rewarded, even if the efforts did not always translate into improved sales. Ed Rensi commented on the commitment he made to the entire organization one time, when sales and morale were at a low point. "I sent 35,000 tins of popcorn. I sent it to managers, the regional offices, and all staff. I said in the letter, 'Sit down with your family and watch television and eat some popcorn.'" This was Ed's way of showing his appreciation to his team members and their families, and fostering further loyalty to the company, so that we continued to push to be the best.

As Peter Drucker, the American management icon, has repeated often: "What gets rewarded, gets done." What could be more simplistic than that?

Food for Thought

Studies show that the top reason people leave their jobs is because they feel disengaged with their work and are not recognized and appreciated for their efforts.

Replacing talent is expensive enough, but it can cost companies even more in lost profits as new replacements are trained and projects are not accepted due to lack of staffing. Companies can cultivate employee loyalty by implementing a recognition program for deserving individuals.

- Educate the entire staff about the program. Be sure that everyone understands what the rewards will be based on. Post the program for all to see, and promote it frequently.
- Develop an ongoing commitment to identify deserving employees.
- Celebrate team efforts that support the company's values and goals. Make sure that all goals have clearly defined measurements that maintain the goals' objective nature.
- Reward both team and individual performance.

Giving Stock

Stock can be the greatest gift of all. McDonald's was one of the first companies to issue stock—a testament to Ray's belief that the company was one in which we would grow together, rewarding those who truly helped build the company. Take Fred Turner. Ray, on his seventieth birthday, gave Fred and Patty

Turner each $1 million in stock. That gift to Patty was a powerful recognition to her role as a spouse.

"Ray was very generous," Fred said recently. "He gave stock to other employees. And when he gave stock to Patty and me, he wanted Patty to get the same amount. He was very conscious of that, and he paid the tax for it."

By issuing that stock to both Fred and Patty, Ray was taking care of family. And that sense of family spilled over into corporate and into the stores, where as peers and mentors we were trained to recognize QSC, and credit employees, at any level, for enhancing the customer experience. We had a lot of tools in our arsenal to give instant recognition on the spot. We were looking for reasons to show our gratitude to people.

Ray's gift to the Turners showed his deep appreciation for Fred's ability to build the company into what it is today. And yet, McDonald's stock was distributed to employees at all levels. Though this practice now must meet with stricter Securities and Exchange Commission guidelines, private companies today may be well served to distribute shares, with the same style for which Ray was legendary, to an extremely deserving right-hand person.

187

Ed Rensi, retired president, remembers Ray's gifts to employees in a number of ways. "When he turned 70 years old, he gave me enough stock that I could buy my first house. What a great and wonderful gift he gave me! Ray Kroc would send us popcorn makers on Father's Day. He would send us umbrellas. He would send us stuff on Mother's Day for the women."

And recognition was not just for the operators or the company employees. Consider Ted Perlman, who started out with his father and has served as a McDonald's supplier for 49 years. Of the recognition his organization receives from the company versus other organizations he is associated with, Ted said: "It's more, just because you're involved more. Here the suppliers have much more of an input and involvement. We just had a conference in Asia, and we got three awards for the outstanding performance we did because there were snowstorms and . . . stores closed because they didn't have supplies. We were able to supply them."

Lesson Learned

Don't just recognize the employee. Recognize his or her significant other. After all, without the support of the employee's partner, he or she would likely never be able to continually deliver such great results.

Recognizing the Front Line

188

Frontline employees are the public face of the company, and they interact with the customer on a level that most people in corporate never experience. But many of McDonald's corporate leaders, in fact, 42 percent of the current worldwide leadership, started out as crew. As a result, their understanding of the rhythm of the operation is what makes the company so strong.

Food for Thought

How many companies today demonstrate respect for their front-line employees?

I am amazed when I walk into well-known chain stores only to find that they have interminable lines at the cashier, and the staff is disengaged with the customer. And there is never a manager in sight. Many people walking into the store turn around and walk right out, not wanting to face those long lines at the register. In my consulting practice today, we call this missed opportunities.

At McDonald's, when the lines started to grow, we'd open another register. Think of this in today's competitive business climate. In the fast-food industry, it is worthwhile to pay a person's $10 hourly wage (use a realistic average) and ring up an extra $100 or more in sales. But consider other retailers, such as in the home-improvement sector, where the average customer receipt could be as high as $70. You're still paying that $10 hourly wage, but the register is ringing up even bigger sales. It is investment spending of the highest order. Do the math.

Of course, you can't bring someone in for a one-hour shift to handle a peak hour for sales. So you bring in someone for a four-hour shift . . . you're still ahead. Enhance that strategy with a recognition program, and you are bound to build loyalty with both your employees and your customers. Quality and speed of service are uncommon in most retail businesses today. Stand out.

189

"If we worked in a McDonald's ourselves as crew, it was indelible," Fred Turner recently told me, when commenting about leadership skills within the company. "We had every respect for those working crew."

Learning to Hustle

Back in 1966, I discovered this culture at McDonald's without really understanding it when I first started there at age 16 working crew. At the time, I fretted over whether I had the skills to succeed. Many of the items that today are ready-to-serve then required manual preparation by the crew. We were in a fishbowl, in the old red-and-white style buildings designed to let the public see just what went on behind the scenes in the kitchen. There were even benches on the outside so that customers could sit and watch the crew at work, and see how clean our operation was—an important mission at a time when some were skeptical about how good a 15-cent hamburger really was.

Crew jobs at McDonald's have long been dismissed as menial jobs, but in reality, these employees had the opportunity to grow into the system and move up. The system is designed to spot hardworking talent, from the moment of hire. Work hard, and someone will notice. Work hard, and there will be a potential opportunity. So I made the conscious effort to perform at my very best, even though I knew very little about making hamburgers, let alone how to handle a busy lunch crowd.

190

"Hustle!" Ralph, my manager, shouted this command regularly. He was a man of few words, but hustle was definitely one of them. Anytime Ralph shouted "Hustle!" we sprung into action, literally running from station to station, serving the customers. Each job depended on the other and collectively personified teamwork. If one worker did not keep up, inevitably a backlog would result, causing lines to sometimes stretch out to the street—a definite taboo. As the newcomer to the team, I was fairly intimidated. What if I could not keep up? I had images of that *I Love Lucy* episode, where Lucy works at a candy factory but falls behind in production. How embarrassing it would be to let the team down, especially in front of all the customers!

I listened carefully to my assigned trainer, the "star" bun man in the store, awed by his peers for his ability to keep up with demand, no matter how big the lunch rush. I strove to place the buns gently on the grill—no thumbprints on the crowns! —and serve them up on a tray, where I'd next dress them, adding cheese when the bin person called for it.

Overwhelmed, I got through my initial fumbling, dropping the spatula noisily on the floor, all eyes watching me, the rookie, messing up. I got a few burns from that 375-degree heat. Still, by the end of my shift, I caught on to the routine. Even the grill-man, the key player in the kitchen orchestrations—the quarterback, admired by the entire crew—took a moment to say, "Paul, you did alright for your first day." I felt like I belonged.

Over time, I realized that early praise was just one part of the system, yet prevalent enough so that even peers commended you for being a valued player.

Suddenly, I was part of a team. And I loved it. Things went well over the next few weeks, but little did I know they were about to get better.

191

Ralph's 5 Cents

After only three weeks on the job, Ralph, the store manager, came over to me on a Saturday, just after the rush, and said he wanted to speak with me on the side. In those tight quarters, not only did you hear almost everything that was said, you also observed what was going on. Any action involving the manager was always under surveillance. So during my journey to the side of the store by the back wall, probably about 10 feet at the most, I had numerous sets of eyes on me.

"I'm very impressed with your 'hustle,'" Ralph told me. "So, I'm giving you a nickel raise to $1.30."

Wow. As a teenager working my first real job, a raise was actually foreign to me. But the way Ralph delivered it, I felt so appreciated, I would have done anything for Ralph, the McDonald's store, or the organization. With my peers watching, I thanked Ralph and walked back to my spot with newfound pride, my frame a bit taller, my chest pushed out a bit. Years later, others, including a former division president, expressed similar emotions about their promotions. So it wasn't just the first-time employees who became so impressed about receiving a raise.

Lesson Learned

Small gestures can go a long way in giving recognition to individuals. Recognition leads to improved engagement and motivation. We can always do more.

The Power of Public Praise

Small gestures delivered in a big way positively influence the restaurant floor. This was evident at one of my New York stores, where I served as director of operations for a franchisee. Rich, one of the managers, was a stern individual who at times led his operation with an iron fist. But his crew also greatly respected his leadership abilities. One Saturday I witnessed why.

It was just after the lunch rush, and the store was a beehive of activity, with crew sweeping, mopping, filling up the ice-bins—all of the tasks necessary to get the store back in shape, ready for the next onslaught of customers. I noticed Rich, his eyes constantly on the flow of activity and the customers, rather loudly call for a worker at the counter area to "come back and see me now." The moment had the earmarks of a very strong reprimand; every employee in the store watched while this particular worker walked over to Rich, no doubt pondering what was next for her. Rich asked her to bring her timecard to him— again, not a good sign. But Rich had another agenda.

As soon as she brought him the card, Rich declared in the same strong voice for all to hear, "What an outstanding job you've done the last few hours. From your speed of service [she'd brought in more money than any of the other counter crew] to the smile and attentiveness you gave your customers—it was just outstanding. I wanted to thank you personally. I'm writing in the rest of your hours for today. So go home and take the rest of the day off. With pay."

Well, you couldn't have imagined the buzz among the crew. And for good reason. Public praise for those who meet your high standards snaps everyone to attention. Rich, I am reasonably certain, hadn't read about this approach in a management book. Yet, as a part of the McDonald's system, instinctively, he had absorbed the kind of management style that generated results and knew what would work. And he wasn't afraid to try something different, while at the same time kept within McDonald's parameters of always striving for QSC. This is part of the very formula for McDonald's growth. No wonder Rich was so successful with his people.

Recognition: The Great Motivator

The formula had always been simple. Work hard, prove yourself, and you were bound to receive recognition. It was a common thread throughout McDonald's. Many of us sought that praise—whether it was because we never received it growing up, because some of us felt the need to prove ourselves, or because we got turned on when representing the organization with pride as we pushed up our shirtsleeves and made it happen every day.

Recognition left its mark, and it's a tool many of us carried into our post-McDonald's life. Willis Smart, now an operations vice president with Dunkin Brands, said to me, "I just talked about this [recognition] at a team meeting about three weeks ago. About the pride of doing things right and how easy it is to recognize and make people feel good about their work."

There was a deep-seated motivation for recognition, and this we won through the surrogate family within the store. We also learned to give recognition as much as we loved to receive it. And we pushed on. Barriers were dropped. We found a niche, and the entry fee was performance. Pedigree didn't matter, and neither did gender, color, or age. All you had to do was deliver, and you were accepted. What company couldn't prosper from that?

To this day, McDonald's thrives on diversity. The company has the largest number of minority and female franchisees in the quick-service industry. More than 40 percent of all McDonald's U.S. owner/operators are women and minorities. And the company consistently wins awards as the best place to work.

Public recognition was the great motivator within all levels of McDonald's. Not only did it successfully serve to reward the conscientious employee, it also helped raise the bar across the board. If a peer won an award for working on a committee, cutting costs, or improving customer service, and you didn't, well, it was obvious why. Awards and celebrations were a part of the fiber at the national level, inspiring regional leaders to do the same locally. Their enthusiasm spilled over to forward-thinking owner/operators, who in addition to following the McDonald's system, applied their creativity within their own units to motivate managers and crew.

In 1988, McDonald's created its most prestigious award, the "Freddy," an award exclusively for top management. Taken as a nod to the Emmys and the Oscars of Hollywood fame, the idea was to honor the spirit of Fred Turner, reflecting his qualities of "unparalleled integrity, strength, vision, and mastery of McDonald's basics." As a recipient of the award, I can say winning it was quite an honor, and one by which I was completely taken aback, as it had only been given out twice before. To be selected in that group was a real thrill, and once again it showed the recognition that the system continued to instill in its culture.

Meaningful Rewards

Recognition worked because it was meaningful. Operators with top-performing stores, for instance, were given consideration to open other stores, as John Cooke, a former senior vice president, reminded me. And generally, these stores ended up being the higher-sales-volume and higher-profit stores. The best operators want to be recognized as such, and what better way to say it than with the highly sought-after chance to open a new store?

Tony Liedtke, a multiple-store operator from Long Island, has been using different forms of recognition for his managers and crews for years, and with great results. "I think recognition is the key," Tony said. "McDonald's is a people business and you cannot have good people and not recognize them. When I give something to my folks, I always make it for a specific purpose. If I am sending you out to dinner, I will find out your favorite restaurant, or your wife's favorite restaurant. I had someone do a great presentation for me one time, and I asked them where they would like to go that they had never been. So I sent them to a Caribbean island. I want the "wow" factor. One time one of my key managers, she is now a supervisor, had really been working hard—working late hours, never home, the whole deal. I wanted to do something for her as well as for her husband and son. I found out that the husband and son were big Yankee fans. I got them some super seats for the two of them. I sent them to the husband and let him know how much I appreciate the job his wife has been doing and for the two of them to cheer on the Yankees. I later received a handwritten note from the son. I find the key to recognition is to show that you are really sincere about it, and the way you show that is to give them something that they don't expect."

195

One on One with Frank Behan

It's one thing to give recognition to those who deserve it. But it's equally important to encourage those who are bypassed so that they stay engaged with the system. Frank Behan said he made it a point to lay the groundwork for future success for those who were bypassed in favor of a higher achiever. As an example, he recalled the instances where only one out of three possible operators would be granted the license for a new store in a particular territory. He took the time to call the ones who were not selected to say, "I can't give it to you. You're a nice guy, but you didn't earn it, and it wouldn't be right. Look, I feel terrible, and it's nothing personal." In many instances the operators would strive to turn circumstances around so they wouldn't lose out again or disappoint Frank. Frank's approach emphasizes the importance of supporting the other talent in an organization—not just the immediate winners. Not all of the executives followed Frank's script, but they still made the effort to spell out the action steps so that a strong contender always stood the chance to achieve.

Lesson Learned

Make recognition meaningful to employees. While a bonus might be nice, time off might be more appreciated by, say, a mom or pop who wants to spend time with the kids. Others may savor the kind of event they might not treat themselves to otherwise—find out if they like theater or concerts, and give them orchestra seats and a gift certificate to a nearby restaurant. Look for the opportunity to impress.

Praise from Ray Kroc Himself

Certainly, on the corporate level we were encouraged to try different approaches, all in the name of being the best, though sometimes other conflicts ensued. For instance, back when I worked as a training manager, I wanted to get my staff more field oriented, and get them visible in the field rather than only conducting "classes" for managers and assistant managers. Along with my four-person staff, we began to visit stores. In truth, this was not a regular practice for the training department. Rather, it was the responsibility of the field service group, which made store visits and graded operators accordingly. This developed into a bit of a discord with field service, and I reached into my growing bag of tricks to navigate this issue. Once I explained to the field service staff that we were merely augmenting their visits and supporting their direction, things got better, and the two departments started a working relationship that became a real positive force.

That kind of push helped our department to win many accolades, and that year I was fortunate to receive the President's Award. This was my first opportunity to receive recognition on a corporate level. And it was heady stuff. This was given to roughly 1 percent of the entire employees, and the process of review had to go all the way up to the president of the company for approval.

In typical McDonald's fashion a beautiful award and a stock option grant was given. Perhaps the best reward was the dinner organized in Chicago. At this gala, Ray Kroc personally gave us our awards, and then to the delight of everybody there, he proceeded to play the piano for us, much the way a relative would at a holiday gathering. He also shook everyone's hand and autographed copies of his book, *Grinding It Out*. It was a memorable time that again showed me the power of recognition—and made me feel that the people and company to which I devoted myself cared about me. And it showed how the top people could have such impact on the folks in the field. It was a thrill to meet Ray for the first time and have a chance to speak with him. I began to realize just how big this organization was, but how small they kept the feeling of family. And I sure felt a part of the family of McDonald's.

One on One with Fred Turner

In interviewing Fred Turner for this book, I was privileged to spend several days with him. If we were in the car and he got a phone call, he'd ask the caller to guess who he was with, and after a few seconds, say, "Paul Facella," and hand me the phone to say hello. Maybe two of the callers really knew who I was. Other times, he insisted upon introducing me as his "senior partner" to the folks he knew. My knee-jerk reaction was, "Fred, Ray was your senior partner, not me." He just smiled at me on that. It's not like Fred really thinks I'm his senior partner. Yet, he made me feel special. Here I am with one of the legends of the company, and he's calling me his partner. For Fred, there still is no class distinction. We are all equal, all part of the family. What a way to give recognition!

Lesson Learned

Praise from the top—the very top—is the kind of recognition employees bask in. Give it to those who are truly deserving, and make it a celebration. Encourage the highest levels in your organization to become part of the process of recognition, and make it a ritual. They will enjoy it as well.

The Trickle-Down Effect

I treasured those powerful moments of recognition so much that I brought them into my own region, as a vice president, combining recognition and achievement with direction and clear vision. Much like the awards programs conducted in corporate, I ran state-of-the-region events that were gala affairs where I discussed what we accomplished in the previous year, and the direction and the goals we would shoot for in the year to come. And in my presentation, I made a point of recognizing the efforts of top-performing operators by name—either in a speech or through visual images projected during the event. With a nod to the corporate awards program, we launched an annual yearbook for the operators and staff. The idea was simple enough: Take the concept of a high school yearbook and replicate it each year. We took portraits of all the operators, and assembled them in the yearbook in chronological order, from the time they came into the system. We also included which committees they served on and the awards they received during their career, similar to the way sports and clubs are presented in high school editions. This gave those senior operators some pride in their seniority and also provided everyone an equal opportunity to show their commitment to the region, by listing their activities.

The book also featured plenty of pictures of events during the year as well as any awards and recognition of our operators and staff. All store awards—and we gave many— were highlighted, as were new stores and remodels and the "regional records" for sales in the hour, day, and annual categories, as well as stores that had the highest percentage of drive-thru business. These became "badges of honor" for all the awardees.

Those who hadn't received such honors could easily grasp why not. In almost every instance, they belonged to few, if any, committees. In all likelihood, they hadn't remodeled, and they hadn't broken any regional records. To do that, you needed "fire in the belly"—the kind that Ray Kroc and Fred Turner built McDonald's with. Still, they were encouraged to try again.

> ## Lesson Learned
>
> Public praise given to top performers raises the bar for
> everyone. It allows everyone to see what it takes to get such
> notice—and if they crave it too, they can step up their game. It
> is a win for them, and a win for the company.

The yearbooks and galas were also a perfect venue to promote the region's goals and objectives for the year. To make our
goals attainable, we highlighted the action steps and how we
would measure them. This leveled the playing field for next year,
where everyone had a shot at winning recognition. And most
everyone did.

We even went as far as to recognize a manager of the year,
highlighting him or her at the annual managers' convention and
in the yearbook. Imagine that, a manager, often no older than
his or her early twenties, given incredible recognition for the
year's accomplishments, in a ceremony where the winner
received a National Football League–style ring. The presentation included a drumroll and spotlight as hundreds of people—
be it peers or higher-ups, those from the local region—looked
on. There was no mistaking how much we valued high performance at the store level.

At the end of the yearbook, we listed our goals for the upcoming year in the hopes it would continue to remind everyone of
our direction for the future. Again, it was a simple idea that had
a lot of benefits.

The yearbooks were a big hit—a program that was fun to
implement and also affordable (with today's desktop technology, they are infinitely less costly). They garnered fantastic
results. Challenge your staff (and, in our case, franchisees as
well) to do their best, and they will strive for excellence, engaging their supervisors, managers, and crew to do the same. That

collective competitiveness translated into increased growth for the region, bringing us revenues that far exceeded the national average, landing within the top three in almost every category for many years.

Interestingly, the corporation years later did a company "Superstars" yearbook, which not only showcased individuals who were considered the best of the best in company store operations (I was proud to be in that elite group) in a yearbook style, but also had "playing cards" made up, just like ball players, with stats and other trivia on them. It was a clever attempt once again to give recognition to the staff, and it can be easily adapted to fit any organization.

The galas, spotlights, rings, and yearbooks—none of it amounts to rocket science. And yet it worked because we kept the strategy simple and the programs were well executed and conducted consistently.

Food for Thought

How can you motivate employees to improve performance?

Consider the values that are most important to your organization. Jot down the kind of effort needed to bring those values from the abstract to the concrete. Build those efforts into job descriptions so that employees become accountable for the action steps. Recognize those who achieve the best results, whether by praising them in public, or giving a keepsake at a company celebration, complete with a speech about the employees commitment to excellence, and the results it brought to the organization as a whole. Their peers will see what excellence is all about.

Recognition: The Gift That Gives Back

Always a student of top performance, I was intrigued with why some operators fared better than others. I had my accounting team analyze the top-performing restaurants within my region and noticed this: The successful franchisees shared some commonalities. They consistently developed great people within their organization. They paid more for their people in salary, bonuses, and perks. They understood that to keep and engage employees their compensation package had to be competitive. And they knew that spending a little bit more for talented management readily paid for itself in elevated operational levels, sales, and profits. They knew that simply throwing cash at staff would result in a huge waste of money. So they were more responsive than others about offering raises and bonuses, and provided a culture that kept employees engaged. They offered incentives that were tied to performance. And they utilized celebrations, dinners, awards, and recognition on an ongoing basis. They cultivated a strong social network within the stores, which sometimes even resembled a family unit, strengthening their teams as a whole. Most of their employees had no previous job experience. Yet, the operators saw this as a chance to inspire and engage these first-time workers—and it made a difference in their stores' performance. These operators demonstrated strategies that are useful not just on the restaurant floor but in any business environment.

Lesson Learned

Most employees make no distinction between their immediate manager and the company; hence, the expression "people leave managers, not companies." Recognition must come from all levels of supervision.

Verbal Praise from the Top Trumps All

In most instances, the bigger the organization, the better it can deliver the "wow" factor. But here, too, you can make an impact without a big cash outlay. I will never forget, for instance, my promotion to assistant vice president, when Ray Kroc personally called to offer his congratulations on speakerphone as I stood in a roomful of McDonald's officers. Think about it. A congratulatory phone call from the man who revolutionized the food service industry. That perhaps is recognition in its highest form. The company also treated my wife, Maureen, and me to a weekend in picturesque Lake Geneva, not far from McDonald's Oak Brook, Illinois, home office. Recognition. Done with class.

Spontaneous Recognition

Recognition was so pervasive throughout McDonald's that leadership seemingly seized any opportunity to make a dedicated worker feel valued. Back when I was an assistant manager, for example, I took my future wife to a restaurant for a dinner I could barely afford on my modest salary. Whom do I see over at the corner table, but my owner/operator and his wife. Uncomfortable with what to do, I waved to him sheepishly. We finished our dinner, and as we went to pay the check, the waiter informed me that the "gentleman at the corner table had taken care of it."

That was a very impressionable event in my young life. My feelings about the company and my relationship were transformed yet again. It was a moment (and as I've said, there were many) where I felt that I would do anything for the company. It was one more example of the value McDonald's places on the importance of spousal support. Spouses play a big role in the success of owner/operators and management, and they deserve recognition too.

Recognizing a Legacy

Recognition, as it became apparent in my conversations with so many individuals associated with the McDonald's system, was a huge building block in the company's success. Even Fred Turner succumbed to the personal satisfaction he gained from recognition. "I had the great honor of being told there was a Fred L. Turner Training Center," he told me. "I loved being honored in that way. It came from Jim Cantalupo [the CEO who tragically passed away the night before the annual operator convention]. So, what a generous, thoughtful thing he did. I love it. I'm proud of it." And then, in his usual humble manner he continued, "But, thank God, nobody calls it that. It doesn't bother me a bit. It's Hamburger University."

A Final Thought

Did McDonald's succeed in inspiring each and every employee with its larger-than-life recognition platform? Of course not. Some never received rewards. Some never got the new stores, the next promotion they sought, or, in the case of suppliers, the new territory that was available. These were the people who, for whatever reason, perhaps did not share the same value sets that were expected. The system was designed to weed out these individuals who ultimately realized, in the words of *From Good to Great* author Jim Collins, that it was time to "get off the bus." This, I'm sure, was tough on these individuals, and it was not easy either for their superiors who had the responsibility to hold onto the standards of the brand (see Chapter 5).

In Summary

The McDonald's system seems to have a built-in mechanism to recognize those who really deliver results. As a rule, the company stays on its toes to retain the best talent at the corporate, store, and vendor level. And the strategy has served McDonald's well, enabling it to choose from within for its top positions. Organizations that develop recognition programs to reward outstanding efforts will have a full roster of its most important resources—their people.

Key Learnings

✔ Build a culture steeped in recognition to reward standout employees and teams, consistently and with clear reasoning.

✔ Train everyone at the company to acknowledge exceptional performance, on the spot. Make it a part of the job to continually praise performance.

✔ Rewards don't have to be costly; employees will appreciate a handwritten note from the top boss or a handshake that accompanies the words "nice job."

✔ Public praise singles out top performers and makes them an example before their peers; it works wonders. Simple ceremonies in the office can be very effective.

✔ Devote a public space at your company for special awards that honor top performers and devoted employees. Keep it current and respectful of the heritage of excellence within the organization.

✔ Make awards meaningful, whether they are promotions, opportunities, or plaques distributed at the holiday gala. Carry out the rituals in a way that's first class.

✔ Develop a feeling of family by including spouses whenever possible in the celebration and recognition.

✔ Ensure that recognition programs are alive and well at your organization by putting in place a specific budget each year for these events and activities.

Epilogue

During the development and research for this book I found the seven principles solidly embraced by those individuals we interviewed. These principles were universally recognized by our interviewees for their role in making the McDonald's system the organization it is today. As mentioned in the introduction, these seven principles may not be new to many readers. What is unusual, however, is the depth and breadth of them and the seriousness that the organization accepted and endorsed them. But we felt there was more.

While the principles set the company's core values, there were also several specific traits and activities that emerged that did not always have clear linkage to the seven principles. In some ways these characteristics made a difference simply because of the luck of timing. In other instances the results attributed to these aspects exemplified the synergy of the individuals at the time, the team effort toward a resolution or a policy, or even the sheer personality of the individuals at the moment. They are part of the components of the success of the system.

Here are six other aspects that helped as well:

1. **The triumvirate.** Ray Kroc, Fred Turner, and Harry Sonneborn: the visionary leader, the disciplined tactical manager, and the

savvy financial expert. These three, although their relationships were tested in the early years, proved to be an incredibly potent leadership team. Arguably, they never would have accomplished all that they did without June Martino, officially Ray's secretary, and later both corporate secretary and treasurer, who in many ways was the glue that kept this early group together. The personalities and styles of the triumvirate were very different and led to some heated arguments and fights between the three, with the near departure of Fred Turner at one point. Credit also must go to Don Conley, the first franchising vice president, and to Jim Schindler, who led kitchen design and engineering. These six individuals from the very beginning proved to be a powerful group whose synergy was unbounded. And the motivation, springing from Ray himself, led them to believe that they were on a mission of noble proportions. They not only made many important decisions early on but also established the grounding principles and core values that the organization would hold perpetually in highest regard.

2. **Meritocracy**. The organization was, and still is, built on a model of performance-based promotions. The ability to attract talented people who desire the rush of being held accountable and the latitude to make decisions is a deep culture within the system. In my interviews for this book, sources repeatedly showed a gratitude for the *opportunity* they were given at McDonald's that was based clearly on their ability to achieve a specific goal—that opportunity, coupled with their passion to thrive, seemed to serve as an aphrodisiac to many in the company. This was true for both vendors and licensees as well. While backgrounds and pedigrees were not a concern, what mattered most were a universal work ethic and a drive to excel. It wasn't about the right skills; it was about *the right values*. Clearly, reinforcing the message of performance were those ubiquitous

reward programs and recognition tools: the simple dinners, the stock options, the promotions, and much, much more.

3. **Three-legged stool.** This concept, totally without peer in its early inception, and still unique today, is a symbol of the integrity and relationships that run deep with all three of the legs: owner/operator, supplier, and corporate staff. The word *partner* came up in numerous conversations, and although it may be a stretch to use that term literally, the point was evident. Few, if any, organizations adopt the McDonald's style of nurturing the mutual respect and interdependence that go beyond the superficial. Ray Kroc, however, saw that these kinds of partnerships are the very key to developing a mutually successful business system that synergizes all parties.

4. **Franchise model.** The system thrived on the full-time, best efforts of all licensees. The model is based on the belief in the individual store operating independently but dependent on the strength of the system. Territories were never given away to corporate partners. Instead, the system relied on individual entrepreneurs. This seemingly innocuous aspect—requiring full-time operators committed to their restaurants and on premise—was a clear advantage. The system needed working, hands-on franchisees, and there was no way to dodge that requirement, so individuals who sought the "quick buck" and easy dollars never made it to the interview in the first place.

But there was another very important distinction: the financial model that Harry Sonneborn developed. While Ray had shunned many of the methods that a franchisor turned to in order to generate income, he had not thought about what might replace it. Harry came in with the novel approach of leasing the real estate back to the franchisee, with a markup, effectively making McDonald's the owner of one of the largest portfolios of real estate in America. It also aligned the interests of both the franchisor and the franchisee, as the incentive was to improve sales, which would effectively configure the rent in a "percentage rent" rather than a minimum base rent. It allowed the full clout of McDonald's behind every real estate transaction, unlike most franchises, which had the independent operator signing the leases and negotiating the deals. This was very appealing to landlords and owners of property. They understood the McDonald's name far better than they did an individual franchisee. And, this arrangement provided McDonald's with a steady income stream over the course of the lease and license, which was normally 20 years.

5. **Never satisfied.** McDonald's thrives on its deeply driven culture of always striving to improve. Even the most recent McDonald's convention used the word *imagine* as its theme. That certainly conjures up the idea of stretching to try new things. The system has always pushed for continuous learning and innovation. The restless energy to be quicker, faster, better, and hotter has been nurtured in the culture of McDonald's since its inception. It has appealed to many employees, who readily enjoyed the constant drive to challenge and improve the system. It gave a sense of empowerment that "we can do it best," and that only the best vendors, staff, and efforts will suffice. It helped to nurture an esprit de corps that helped propel the organization and many of its staff to great accomplishments.

It also belies another important point: the obsession with operational excellence. Few competitors over the years looked to the degree to which *how the stores operated* to such an extreme obsession. Perhaps this fixation was part of Fred Turner's famed intensity. From a fanatical attention to the smallest details of operations, to the millions spent on training and developing of management candidates, the company never lost its focus—that the individual restaurant serving a customer, the moment of truth, was the most important measurement of its success. And that was everyone's mission—to make that connection with the customer the best possible experience.

6. **Heritage.** Ray was involved with the system till he died at age 81 in 1984. Fred has been active his entire McDonald's career. No organization can boast of a more involved group of founders that continue the tradition. Consider for example, James McLamore, a Cornell graduate who cofounded Burger King in 1954, Dave Thomas, who founded Wendy's in 1969, Wilbur Hardee, a founder of Hardee's, and Glen Bell, who founded Taco Bell in 1962, all sold out in later years.

Of the five organizations, McDonald's clearly emerged as the leader by any method of comparison, and I submit that the heritage of the McDonald's system is a part of the reason why. At Burger King, within 13 years of its founding, it was sold, though James McLamore stayed on as president until 1970 and chairman until 1976. In Wendy's case, Dave left after 13 years, in 1982, and then came back to the ailing company to assist in marketing in 1986. At McDonald's, however, Ray's consistent presence until the day he died meant the system benefited from a total of 29 years of his continuous involvement. And, of course, his legend and legacy has been kept alive admirably by the company, in numerous ways. Fred has been very much a part of the fabric of the organization for the full 53 years of its existence, and he still maintains an office on the McDonald's campus, and the title honorary chairman. Both men gave their entire remaining business lives to the company, and the company has never been without the involvement of a spiritual founder, nor been sold or acquired.

I was a guest at a recent "Ray Kroc Awards" dinner where the top managers around the country were invited to a weekend in Chicago and were lavishly treated to a number of activities over a three-day period. Watching the festivities, which included entertainment and an awards presentation, it was hard not to notice what the real thrill seemed to be for these eager managers. It was having a picture with Fred. Off to the side of the stage, with an infectious grin, was Fred, completely comfortable and having fun chatting with these managers and posing for pictures with them. He was clearly having as good a time as they were. And that was powerful and meaningful to them. It reminded me of my own photo session as a young President's Award winner, in Chicago, some 32 years earlier, having the same feelings of pride and, yes, thrill at meeting the legendary founder himself. It was, to use the well-known phrase, "priceless."

212

The combined total of both Burger King and Wendy's founders is 51 years of involvement; Ray and Fred together equal 82 years and counting. This continuous involvement by the founding individuals is unique in the corporate world. It also is unique in its ability to project stability and grounding, which underscores the values and principles from the very beginning. That unwavering interest says, in effect, "I love this business so much, that I want to stay involved, and help any way I can." Clearly, Fred and Ray, like so many other founders, could have gotten out and retired to the country clubs. That never happened. That is an unusual trait in the current corporate environment of getting in and selling out quickly for as much cash as possible. Ray and Fred have become heroes to the organization, and the fact that they were so available and accessible only added to their legacy. The influence of this is hard to measure, but again, it is one of the aspects that makes the McDonald's system so unique.

The obvious question I heard while writing this book was, "Could the success of McDonald's ever be duplicated?" It's a valid and interesting question. Clearly, the business climate is much different from what Ray and Fred and others found in the 1950s. Today, we are a much more litigious society, and probably more cynical as well. With corporate scandals in the news on any given day, it seems that honesty and trust have become so suspect. What's more, much of what has been written on the newest generation to hit the job market has not been complimentary in regards to the work ethic and commitment to their respective employers.

Yet, despite in these uncertain times, with volatile markets and sweeping layoffs and when people may feel discouraged about the ability to make a difference in the workplace, there remains the potential for positive change. But it can only happen when leaders return to values—the kinds of values that drove McDonald's to the global power it is today. Whether you run a global corporation, a region, a division, a five-person team, or a small business, these values apply. Develop your team to serve as real partners, and together you will achieve more than you otherwise could have on your own.

I believe that the values, principles, and core culture that became McDonald's are universal, in general. More than 53 years and three generations later, these traits have survived and changed with the flow of both the business culture as well as the needs and desires of consumers. So, one could argue, these characteristics have stood the test of time. But more importantly, these qualities, while perhaps not modeled as frequently as in the past, are still evident and still have impact. Those who work within the McDonald's system, for the most part, enjoy what they do, feel good about the product and services they perform, challenge each other to continue to improve, and find both reward and satisfaction in accomplishing these activities. That's universal. And these qualities can be applied to any size organization, group, or company. What's more, they restore an element largely missing in business today: fun in the workplace. When people like what they do, their potential is limitless.

Fred Turner, in April 2008, at the Worldwide Convention, made a statement that sums up the best of those ideals:

> *Who are we? How did we get here? 50 years a blur. . . .*
> *Who do we thank for the ride? Not me, not you, not Ronald.*
> *The company didn't make the operators, the operators didn't*
> *make the company, ditto the suppliers. We made each other,*
> *the three-legged stool.*

I suggest to everyone: Find your own three-legged stool. Find those folks who are the key drivers to your organization and do everything you can to make them, feel, act, and be . . . your partner.

Index

About the Author

PAUL FACELLA is president and CEO of Inside Management Ltd., a New York based management consultancy that counsels organizations from small businesses to Fortune 500 companies in corporate sectors, as well as non-profit and government organizations, in the United States and throughout the world. Additionally, Inside Management is a provider of outstanding training through its national award-winning programs.

At age 16 while still in high school, Mr. Facella began working behind the counter at McDonald's and with the exception of one year's absence, had never left the company until he ventured out on his own 34 years later. Beginning as a Crew Member, he rose through the ranks to positions of increased responsibility including assistant manager, store manager, director of training, and director of operations for a 12-store franchise.

In 1974 he began working for the corporate office as a training manager in the New Jersey region, with promotions to field service manager, director of operations and assistant vice president by 1983. In 1988, Mr. Facella was named regional vice president of the New York Region, a position he held for 12 years. Under his leadership, the New York region experienced a four-fold increase in profit and a 90 percent increase in store count, achieving an unprecedented $600 million in revenue, described by the Northeast Division president as "one of the strongest performing regions in the country."

He is a past board chairman and served for 20 years as an active member of the New York Urban League and has served on the boards of the United Way of Long Island, the Nassau County Youth Program, Ronald McDonald House of New York, Citykids of NYC, Ronald McDonald Children's Charities, Happy Talkers, and Happy House organizations. He is a lifetime member of the National Eagle Scout Association and has a 38-year involvement with his local volunteer fire department.

He and his wife, Maureen, reside in Long Island, New York and enjoy vacationing in Vermont, and he has a long-time hobby of automobile racing. They have three grown children in the New York area.

Mr. Facella is currently an entrepreneur in a number of business ventures and is eager to help you bring the 7 principles he learned at McDonald's to your organization. He can be reached by e-mail at AskPaul@insidemanagement.com or through his Web site, www.insidemanagement.com.